PENNSYLVANIA FIRESIDE TALES

VOLUME 6

JEFFREY R. FRAZIER

CATAMOUNT
PRESS

an imprint of Sunbury Press, Inc.
Mechanicsburg, PA USA

CATAMOUNT
PRESS

an imprint of Sunbury Press, Inc.
Mechanicsburg, PA USA

For information about special discounts for bulk purchases, please contact Sunbury Press Orders Dept. at (855) 338-8359 or orders@sunburypress.com.

To request one of our authors for speaking engagements or book signings, please contact Sunbury Press Publicity Dept. at publicity@sunburypress.com.

FIRST CATAMOUNT PRESS EDITION: December 2024

Set in Adobe Garamond | Interior design by Crystal Devine | Cover by Lawrence Knorr | Edited by Debra Reynolds.

Publisher's Cataloging-in-Publication Data
Names: Frazier, Jeffrey R., author.
Title: Pennsylvania fireside tales volume 6 / Jeffrey R. Frazier.
Description: First trade paperback edition. | Mechanicsburg, PA : Catamount Press, 2024.
Summary: Volume 6 in the Pennsylvania Fireside Tales series exploring the origins and foundations of old-time Pennsylvania mountain folktales, legends, and folklore.
Identifiers: ISBN : 979-8-88819-154-5 (paperback).
Subjects: NATURE / Ecosystems & Habitats / Mountains | HISTORY / United States / State & Local / Middle Atlantic (DC, DE, MD, NJ, NY, PA) | FICTION / Fairy Tales, Folk Tales & Mythology.

Designed in the USA
0 1 1 2 3 5 8 13 21 34 55

For the Love of Books!

Cover: Based on a crop from a Pennsylvania farm in Carbon County, painted by Gustav Grunewald in the mid-1800s. Allentown Art Museum, Purchase: Gift of Zenon Hansen, by exchange, 1982. (82.07)

— ALSO BY —
JEFFREY R. FRAZIER

Pennsylvania Fireside Tales Volume I

Pennsylvania Fireside Tales Volume II:
The Black Ghost of Scotia & More Pennsylvania Fireside Tales

Pennsylvania Fireside Tales Volumes III, IV, V, VII, and *VIII*

Pennsylvania Fireside Ghost Tales
(ghost tales from in and around Pennsylvania's state parks and historic sites)

Pennsylvania Mountain Landmark Volumes I–III

Indian Head Rock. Located along Route 42 near the town of Catawissa in Columbia County, this unusual formation is also known locally as Profile Rock. Legend states that it is the profile of a Delaware Indian Chief named Lapachpeton whose village once stood near here. See the chapter entitled "Faces From the Past" in this volume for the sad story of the chief's daughter, whose name, according to the legend, was Minnetunke. Photo: American Views Photography and Post Card Co., 5430 Berwick Road, Bloomsburg, Pennsylvania.

CONTENTS

CONTENTS

Romances such as these have floated down to us as wreck upon the ocean. We gather a fragment here and a fragment there, and at length, it may be, we learn something of the name and character of the vessel when it was freighted with life and obtain a shadowy image of the people who perished.

—Robert Hunt
(Popular Romances of the West of England)

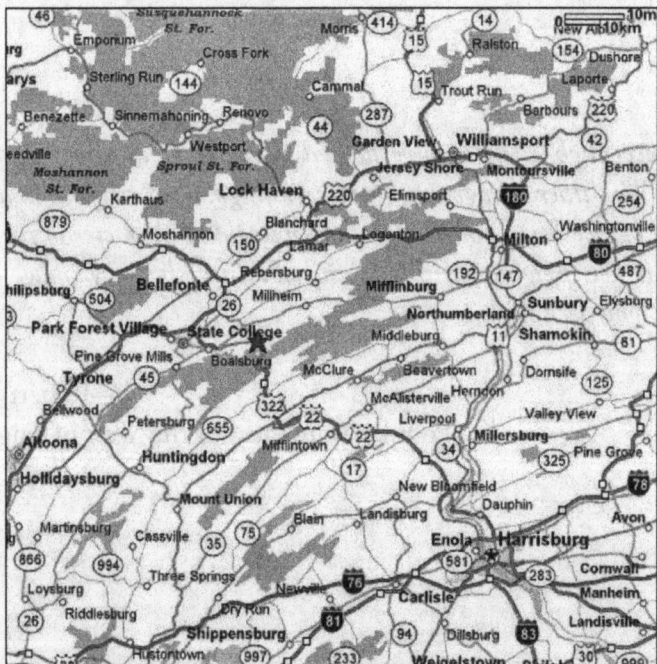

WHERE THE SEVEN MOUNTAINS MEET THE SKY. Map
of the central Pennsylvania region that is the setting for many of the
stories in the Pennsylvania Fireside Tales books.

INTRODUCTION

Over half a century ago I became addicted to the legends and folk-tales of Pennsylvania. I had always liked to hear the old tales, even as a young lad, but I decided to collect them and preserve them in a book or two at that late date. That book or two has extended to eight volumes in a series I've titled *Pennsylvania Fireside Tales*, and, most recently, a three-volume series titled *Pennsylvania Mountain Landmarks*.

After initially self-publishing *Pennsylvania Fireside Tales Volume I*, I continued to find several episodes related to the Indians of Pennsylvania, more ghost witch and supernatural tales, and many of the old-time hunting episodes I liked so much, hence the self-publication of seven more. All eight were self-published as hardbacks, but then in 2023 Sunbury Press offered to publish all eight volumes as paperbacks, along with my new *Pennsylvania Mountain Landmarks Volumes I–III*.

It was an offer I could not refuse, since it established me as a full-fledged commercially published author, and because it would give me a chance to improve all previously self-published volumes by adding and improving photos, correcting and expanding text in each chapter, and working with a publisher which I knew would add a new level of quality to the books.

So, in forthcoming Sunbury Press volumes look for more hunting and Indian episodes, and supernatural stories like that of Clinton County's dancing cupboard, the Ingleby Monster in Centre County, or Spook Hollow in Clearfield County. These latter types always hold a fascination for lovers of the odd and unexplained; so I plan to tell them since, after all, the first story I collected was a story that fell into that category, and such accounts always intrigued me as well, and still do today.

The reason for that is because it was the mountains themselves that always held the greatest appeal for me, and I'm still enchanted by them. They've not only given me their colorful tales but have also provided me with many pleasurable memories of hikes and drives into some of their most beautiful hollows and broadest vistas. As a result, I've developed a few favorite overlooks that I could recommend to the sightseer.

Among those favorites would be Cherry Springs Vista along Route 144 in Potter County, Winkleblech View on Round Top Mountain above Hairy Johns Park in Centre County, Bald Eagle Lookout on Route 15 above Williamsport in Lycoming County, Big Valley view on top of Long Mountain in Mifflin County, and Jo Hays Vista on Tussey Mountain of Centre County. Other Centre County views to which I'm partial are those on Nittany Mountain above Centre Hall, Sky Top on Bald Eagle Mountain above Stormstown, and the view from Rattlesnake Pike on the mountains above Unionville.

There was always something that seemed sacred to me about such places, and I always counted myself lucky when I could visit them. The sight of dark blue mountain ranges in the distance, the green and brown patchwork of fields below, and the outlines of red barns and grey farmhouses snuggled into the rolling hills and forest lands that make the picture complete always reminded me of how fortunate I was. Lucky to be out doing what I loved best; collecting legends and folktales in this green land swept clean by cool mountain breezes.

On the other hand, there is a sweet sadness to the old tales. At one time they are a link with the past, and so satisfy the nostalgic side that all of us have with regards to those who have gone before us. Then at the same time, the tales often hold reminders that life has never been easy, and that all generations, past and present, are linked by a resiliency of the human spirit that can laugh in the face of adversity and pass that same tenacity down to their descendants.

Unfortunately, death has a way of weakening those links, for when an old person dies another door to the past is closed and the path of history grows dimmer because of it. That's why I always felt that it was important to save the old-time anecdotes that were fast disappearing when I started collecting them over fifty years ago.

The job could have been done better if I had been a better writer, had more time to devote to the task, and had more training in the science of folklore. But you do the best you can with the time and resources you've got, especially since no one else seemed ready, willing, or able to take on the challenge.

However, I'd have to say that the biggest frustration for me in writing the stories has been the discovery of particularly interesting facts and details about a story after I'd already written and published it. These sorts of maddening time lapses occurred again and again during the time I was writing all the volumes of the series, and I never felt I had a good opportunity to bring out those types of facts in later volumes. Now I can.

One such example would be the letter I received from a gentleman in Texas who said he was the great great-great-great grandson of Jacob Stanford, who, along with his family, was murdered by Indians near Potters Fort in Centre County in May of 1778. According to this gentleman, one of the Stanford sons was taken captive that day (a fact that somehow escaped the notice of historians), but later escaped and went on to raise a family of his own. It was from this man that my correspondent said he was descended, and had I had this information in hand at the time I initially wrote the story of the massacre (see the story titled "The Lower Fort" in Volume II), it would have added a nice touch to the chapter.

Regardless of all those kinds of aforementioned frustrations and deficiencies in the tales, many folks have nonetheless enjoyed my efforts; and I have appreciated, and will continue to do so, comments from readers—especially those who may wish to provide me with tales for additional volumes I may write one day. My phone is 814-360-4401; my email: Jandhfra2@yahoo.com; and my postal address: 100 Hawknest Way–Apt. 135, Bellefonte, Pa. 16823. You can also contact me or order books through my website at www.pafolktales.com or through my publisher at SunburyPress. com. Lastly, I'd like to thank my son James for the drawings that appear in this and in previous volumes.

Jeffrey R. Frazier

AUTHOR'S NOTE

The preceding paragraphs are what appeared in previous editions of this volume, and the same chapters that appear in this new Sunbury Press edition are the same ones that were included in the previous editions plus a new chapter. There are also additions to the original chapters. These extras include interesting details that were not discovered until after the previous editions were published and which I felt needed to be added to the chapters in order to enhance their quality. This edition has all the original photos that appeared in past editions plus many new ones. The author hopes they add a whole new level of interest to the original tales and also add to the reader's enjoyment.

CHAPTER I

PERILS OF THE PATH

When the deserted Cameron House Hotel burned to the ground sometime in the second or third decade of the twentieth century, many locals thought the fire also finally laid its ghost. Business at the hotel had begun to decline as the lumber kings cleaned out the remaining stands of virgin hemlocks in the Black Forest of Cameron, Elk, and Potter Counties in the 1890s, and most people attributed the slide in the Cameron House's business to the area's decline in employment.

There were some, however, who averred that the hotel's falling fortunes were not because of a lack of jobs in the neighborhood, but because the old building was just too haunted; its ghost, they said, had scared off too many paying guests over the years, until its reputation as a haunted hotel was enough to discourage all but the bravest souls from staying there.

Certainly there were enough people who could attest to that fact, including the bark peelers, teamsters, lumber camp cooks, sawmill workers, and local brick plant employees, who had stayed at the hotel at one time or another and who had either seen the apparition themselves, or knew someone else who had. Nonetheless, for whatever the reason, by the 1920s the hotel had been abandoned.

Those who remembered seeing the old frame structure, which was located near the present-day community of Cameron in Cameron County, described it as a "pretty good-sized building,"[1] but a somber-looking place. Even the large red block letters forming the words CAMERON HOUSE on the upper front half of its blackened wooden siding did little to give the

---

1. George Tibbens (born 1913), recorded August 14, 1999.

place a genteel look. Working against that was the hotel's isolated location and the dense woods around it, both of which were enough to convey an impression that it was a lonely and depressing spot.

But even worse, on certain blustery days and nights, the wind, sounding like a long-suffering soul whispering in the hemlocks of the nearby forest and wailing under the eaves of the tin roof, would keep dark clouds, leaves, and dried grasses in constant motion, making the old place seem that much more uninviting. There were many, on the other hand, who were convinced that the eerie sounds that seemed to emanate from the building on occasion, were not caused by the wind but were indeed the sounds of the hotel's ghostly tenant. Counted among those who held that conviction was a local sawmill worker who, after an encounter with the Cameron House's mischievous ghost, vowed he would never stay in the haunted hotel again.

Dalfus Tibbens had come to Cameron County in 1898 to work in a lumber company's sawmill that was, as its workers would say, "cuttin' big timber" in the virgin Black Forest of Cameron County. After a hard first day on the job the weary lumberman was looking forward to a good night's rest in a comfortable bed, and so Tibbens was glad to get a room in the hotel closest to his place of work.

He was tired, but it was a good tired, as he was fond of saying, because he had put in a good day's labor and felt he had earned his day's wages. He was so tired that ghosts and other supernatural events were probably the furthest things from his mind, as the contented woodsman fell into a deep sleep in the little room he had rented in the Cameron House Hotel.

The exhausted lumberman had not slept too long before he felt the bedcovers lift off the foot of his bed and a tickling sensation creeping across his toes. Then, as the surprised man became fully awake, it seemed as though someone was playing with his feet, tickling and pulling on them. At first, he thought a coworker was trying to play a joke on him, but as his eyes became accustomed to the darkness, he could see no one in the room.

Everything there seemed normal and was just as it had been before he went to bed. His clothes were on the old press-backed wooden chair beside the bed, and his shoes and socks were on the floor under the chair. There

Picture of the Cherry Springs Hotel, Potter County. This old time hotel was probably similar to the Cameron House Hotel in that it too was a lumberman's sleeping place. Figure on the left is old-time Potter County hunter and lumberman Laroy Lyman. (Photo courtesy of Krista Lyman.)

was little else in the room since it was just a spartan accommodation, but now that he was fully awake Tibbens was finally able to see a figure at the foot of his bed.

"It sorta looked like an old bum," said Dalfus Tibbens' son, as he told us the story of the Cameron Hotel's ghost that his father had told to him. Sitting on the old man's front porch in Loganton that fine July afternoon in 1999, we were held spellbound as we listened to this ghost tale and many others he had heard over the years, including those of spooks he had encountered himself.

"It was probably a peddler," continued our storyteller as he described the Cameron House Hotel apparition that his father had seen. "They dressed with sloppy clothes, and a pack on their back," he noted, recalling them from personal experience. "I remember peddlers coming here," said our eighty-six-year-old raconteur. "There were a lot of them around. They came around after the Civil War up until the 1920s. Most of them were Jew peddlers."

"They seem to want ta tell you something, and they can't communicate," said the old man, returning to his ghost story and referring once again to the Cameron Hotel's silent but playful ghost.

Whether the hotel ghost was trying to communicate with Dalfus Tibbens or not, its actions were enough to frighten the young man out of his room.

"He jumped outta bed, grabbed his clothes and stuff, and went outside and dressed," continued Dalfus's son. When he went outside there was something goin' on down the street, and he told one fella what had happened.

"Why," said the man, "there was a peddler killed in that room! They killed him for his pack!"

"He told his landlord at the Cameron Hotel that he had to get another room there; that he didn't want nothin' to do with their ghost. But the landlord wouldn't or couldn't give him another room, so he got out of the place completely!" noted our storyteller as he concluded his ghost story.[2]

Had we taken our leave of the old gentleman that day with just this one story it would have been adequate compensation for the long drive we had made to interview him, but the tale of the Cameron House's murdered peddler had awakened memories of similar tales he had heard in his own neighborhood. They were not pleasant stories, but they did confirm that at least a part of the Cameron House ghost story could be based on fact.

"They claimed that up the valley here that's the reason the old Schrader place up near the Price Cemetery was haunted—that there was a peddler killed there. A man I know said that years after the place had been deserted, he was passing by and heard noises in the barn that sounded like twenty horses pawing around in there.

"He picked up a stone and threw it in, and then it sounded like forty horses. He went to throw another stone, but he said something knocked it out of his hand, so he just got out of there. See, years ago people were hard up, and when a peddler came with nice stuff in his pack and they hadn't the money to pay for it, they done away with him!

"And over here on the Greenbriar Mountain there was a peddler killed. The man that told me this story was a Jew, and one of his friends was missing. I'll bet that's the one that turned up missing. There's a fella that confessed it to my dad. He used to farm down here, and he, his mother-in-law, and another man throwed the peddler down and killed him. They

2. Ibid.

throwed him down the well and throwed rocks on him. He said he could still hear him beggin' for his life. He just killed him for his pack!"[3]

Although it might seem that during the late 1800s and early 1900s an itinerant peddler would not encounter the same menaces in his travels as those dangers confronting Pennsylvania's early Indian traders, Mr. Tibbens' tales indicate otherwise. Apparently life-threatening risks went with both jobs; occupational hazards that historian Charles Hanna, in his work on the state's Indian traders, eloquently describes as "perils of the path."[4] However, in the one case it was the state's native sons that sometimes posed a danger to the merchant peddling his wares, whereas in the second case it was the peddler's own kind that sometimes turned against him. And it is not just Mr. Tibbens' stories that point to that fact. Tales of murdered peddlers have surfaced in other parts of the state as well.

One such story is still told up in the northern part of Schuylkill County, near where Catawissa Creek crosses Route 924 between the villages of Brandonville and Sheppton in the Mahanoy Mountains. Here it is said that there is a lonely grave that is the last resting-place of a peddler who was ambushed and robbed there in 1789. For the princely sum of three cents, the bandit took the peddler's life and then buried him on the spot.

Now, locals say, on the anniversary of his death the ghostly form of the murdered man and his horse can be seen at night as they rise from the forgotten grave. The ghostly duo pauses for only a short while, as though looking around for the thief that took the peddler's life. Then suddenly the ghost supposedly screams, falls off the horse, and disappears.[5]

Northumberland County has its tale of a murdered peddler as well. Although not a ghostly account, the story does provide more evidence that a peddler's life could sometimes be a dangerous one. According to the area's historical records, a group of workmen, while "engaged in digging the foundation of the foundry" in Shamokin in 1839, uncovered a man's skeleton.[6]

Beside it they found a rusty old pistol and ten silver dollars. After much conjecture it was concluded that the skeleton was that of a peddler from

---

3. Ibid.
4. Charles A. Hanna, *The Wilderness Trail Volume I*, 44.
5. Patrick M. Reynolds, *Strange But True, Incredible Stories About Pennsylvania*, 14.
6. Everts and Stewart, *History of Northumberland County, Pennsylvania*, 86.

neighboring Mahanoy in Schuylkill County, who "had been missing for some years."[7]

Most peddlers were lucky enough to avoid attempts on their lives, but many of them still, in the words of a well-known popular comedian of today, got no respect. One such man was a peddler who decided to bring his pack of "Yankee notions" into the Scotia Iron Works in Centre County one day. Not knowing the difficulties of entering the works by passing under the inclined plane, the peddler was soon doused with a pail of water by pranksters on the tipple above.

Angered by the pranksters' actions, the peddler leaped off his horse and bounded up the steps to confront his tormentors. On his way up he was doused with four or five more buckets of water before giving up and starting back down. To add insult to injury, he was "helped along by yet another pail of water at his back."[8]

Although a peddler's "Yankee notions," consisting of, among other things, "kerchiefs, laces, finger and ear-rings, blue, crimson, and yellow beads, ribbons, tapes, silver-washed and shining thimbles, hair-combs, brushes, needles, buckles, buttons, and bodkins,"[9] were much admired by the country folks who were the peddlers' clientele, it cannot be said that they always held the traveling salesmen in the same regard.

Peddlers sometimes had a reputation for being swindlers—"smooth articles"—who, in the words of one man who professed to know them well, "would work an hour to cheat you out of a 'fipenny bit'" or who "would cheat you out of your horse or your farm if a good chance offered itself."[10] It certainly would be unfair to say that all peddlers fit this mold, but it probably was a peddler with a reputation like this that led to a story of how he was foiled one day during an attempt to rob a farmer and his wife in Centre County.

Itinerant peddlers eventually became friends with many of their customers, relying on them for a place to spend the night and for both supper and then breakfast the next morning. Oftentimes their sleeping spot might only be a bed of hay in the loft of the farmer's barn, but in the case of some families there would be a bed in their homes especially reserved for the traveling merchants.

---

7. Ibid.
8. Harry M. Williams, *The Story of Scotia*, 58.
9. J. C. Furnas, *The Americans, A Social History of the United States*, 23.
10. Ibid.

Of course, a peddler had to be well known and regarded as trustworthy by a farm family before he would be allowed to spend a night in the house, which meant strange peddlers would have to sleep in a cold and drafty barn if they wanted a roof over their heads. One such peddler is recalled in an old fanciful story, which was once told in Centre County.

Sometime shortly after the Civil War it is recalled that a new peddler pulled a two-wheeled cart with a large wooden box on it up to the front porch of a farmhouse in Penn's Valley, Centre County, and knocked on the door. When the farmer came to the door the peddler explained that he needed a place to stay for the night since darkness was now falling, and he had been on the road all day.

He would, he said, be willing to stay in the barn since he was a stranger, but he asked if it would be all right if he could keep his box inside the house. The box, he said, contained his wares, and he didn't "want it to get wet in case of rain." The farmer agreed, and accordingly the box was brought inside.

After supper the peddler retired to the barn, and the lady of the house cleaned up the kitchen. When she was done, she sat down on her favorite rocker in the parlor and closed her eyes. As she rocked back and forth, she could hear the mantle clock ticking contentedly away. It was a soothing sound, which would have eventually lulled her off to sleep except for the fact that she imagined the antique timepiece was trying to say something to her.

Instead of the normal tick-tock cadence she was used to hearing, the farmer's wife began to think she could hear the clock skip a beat, which made it seem as though it were reciting a warning about the box in the kitchen. "Watch that box, Watch that box, Watch that box," were the words she would later swear the clock began repeating to her just as she was dozing off. Eventually the new cadence became so real and so distinct to her that she finally insisted that the peddler's box be opened.

Reluctant at first, the farmer and his sons eventually opened the weather-beaten old box in the kitchen, and much to their surprise they found a man inside. It wasn't hard to figure out that the man was the peddler's accomplice, and the plan had been for him to let himself out of the box and then let the peddler in the house after the farmer and his family were asleep. The two thieves could then have made off with any cash and valuables they could carry away before the family woke up the next morning.[11]

There was an even hardier breed of traveling merchant that traversed the back roads and mountain byways of rural Pennsylvania during the same time period as the peddlers. These men, who might aptly be called the cowboys of the backwoods, could often be seen driving their herds of cattle, sheep, horses, and other livestock from farm to farm, buying and selling as they went along. Much like the peddlers, a drover would be put up for the night sometimes by hospitable farmers, who also would allow him to pasture his livestock in their meadows.

Farmer James Hamilton was one agriculturalist who offered this kind of genial hospitality to drovers who often passed his way. The Hamilton farm near Bellefonte, Centre County, was no doubt a much-heralded destination for the drovers of bygone years, not only because of the comfortable lodging that was offered but because Mr. Hamilton, in addition to his son, had four daughters who would socialize with the drovers and make their stay a pleasant one. A pleasant oral tradition of the Hamilton family to this day maintains that one of the Hamilton daughters "later married the man she had met as a drover in her father's house."[12]

There was also at least one other drover that fell in love with a young mountain girl he met on his travels. In this case the young lady was not a farmer's daughter, but a maid who worked in a large stone inn that catered to overnight guests of all types. In modern times the old mountain hostelry was a popular eating place for years but did not rent rooms to overnight guests.

Then in the 1960s, the owners of what was then known as the Eutaw House in Potters Mills said that they wanted to eventually offer overnight accommodations, but there are others who say the reason they failed to do so is because, not unlike the old Cameron House Hotel, the place was just too haunted.

If true, then one of the ghosts would have to be that of the drover who fell in love with the pretty young maid who worked in the old stagecoach stop sometime in the first two decades following the Civil War.

11. Dorothy C. Meyer, *Legends and Lore of Centre County*, chapter 13.
12. Myrtle Magargel, "The History of Pleasant Gap," 58th installment of series, *Centre Daily Times*, June 17, 18, 1936.

George Foust's Seven Mountains Hotel. This 1883 sketch appears on an old post card. Not be confused with the nearby Eutaw House, this old-time hostelry also once stood in the Seven Mountains of Centre County. It too was a popular stopping over place for lumbermen, drovers, and other travelers of the old Lewistown-Bellefonte Pike, present day Route 322. (Photo courtesy of Charles Braucht.)

The tragic love story begins around 1880 with the death of a young woman near Lewistown in Mifflin County. Although it was in the middle of a severe winter, the decision was made to transport the dead woman's corpse to Centre Hall, Centre County, for burial. Accordingly, the body was loaded on a spring wagon and the mourners started over the Seven Mountains with a team of horses pulling the wagon.

As they got to the top of Broad Mountain near the Centre/Mifflin County line, a heavy snowfall greeted them, and they found it difficult to make progress. As they went on, the snow storm increased in intensity, and by the time they got to the point where, today, a side road leads off to the east to the Seven Mountains Boy Scout Camp, and the Stillhouse Hollow country, they decided they could not go on. The decision then had to be made as to what to do with the dead body on the wagon, and it was decided to bury her a short distance off the roadside.

The Lewistown pike was a busy thoroughfare in those days, even though it was just a dirt road. Among the many travelers that used the highway were peddlers, carrying their packs, and drovers, driving their herds of cattle and horses to back-country destinations.

To these itinerant salesmen, the old stone inn at Potters Mills was a convenient place to lie over for the night, and so the hotel was usually a busy place. In fact, for a young girl the Potters Mills Hotel, as some called it in those days, was an ideal place to meet fellows who were not locals and who had seen more of the world than just the nearby familiar hollows and valleys of the Seven Mountains.

One evening, shortly after the hasty burial of the dead girl along the dirt road over the Seven Mountains, a handsome drover walked into the Potters Mills Hotel and registered to stay for the night. He did not go unnoticed by one of the hotel's maids, who soon had thought of a reason to introduce herself to him.

The two young people hit it off immediately, and by the end of the evening they had agreed they would talk again the next morning. Looking forward to seeing the drover the next day, the country lass went to her bed in one of the hotel's upstairs rooms and fell into a sound sleep.

Sometime in the middle of the night, she was startled awake by muffled noises coming from a room below. Trying not to let the sounds disturb her, she decided to ignore them and soon went right back to sleep. She awoke the next morning and did not think about the unusual disturbance of the previous night again, until she realized the young drover she was looking forward to talking to was no longer around.

She was told by the landlord that the young man had "gotten up and left real early" that morning, an explanation she first accepted. Later, however, when she was given bloody bedclothes to wash and told that one of the guests had had a real bad nosebleed, some disturbing thoughts began to cross her mind.

The mystery of the missing drover would have probably ended then and there, except for the fact that several years later, the puzzled young lady would tell this story to her girlfriends, the oldest daughters of John Zettle, whose mountain homestead was located along the same road which leads to the Seven Mountains Boy Scout Camp today.

Eventually the Zettle sisters told the story to their father and to their younger sister Mariah. Mariah in turn would later pass the tale on to her son, who in turn told it to me, along with an interesting historical footnote, which possibly sheds new light on the drover's mysterious disappearance.

The Eutaw House. Once an old stagecoach stop, it sits empty and unused today in Potters Mills, Centre County. Travelers on the old Bellefonte / Lewistown Pike would lay over here on their travels over the Seven Mountains country.

"This was at a time when Pennsylvania still had lots of native chestnut trees," began Mariah Zettle's son when he sat down with me to tell the story his mother had passed on to him.

"That same morning (the morning when the maid at the Potters Mills Hotel was asked to wash the bloody bedclothes), it being chestnut season, and a rain during the night being just the thing to hasten the opening of the buds and cause the nuts to fall, mom and some of the other children in the family persuaded their dad to take them for chestnuts. They proceeded along the back road to Gharrity's, and on up the mountain to where they knew there were many chestnut trees.

"After a successful nut-gathering session the girls coaxed their father to go just a short distance more to where the girl from Lewistown had been buried several winters before. When they reached the grave, they noticed that the soil on top was all freshly worked and leveled off. This evidently made quite an impression on Grandpa Zettle, but not much significance was attached to it by the kids.

The Eutaw House's haunted staircase. Named for a popular restaurant that once occupied the building, this historic structure is said to be home to many ghosts, including that of a woman in white that haunts the main staircase shown here.

"Later on, he mentioned it to a couple of other people, and then a few years later he was called to the deathbed of the owner or proprietor of the hotel. The dying man told him he had robbed and killed a young 'drovier' (that's the way mom always pronounced it) and buried him on top of the girl in the mountain grave.

"He had never expected anyone to visit the grave so soon after he buried the drover there, and had been worried after finding out Grandpa Zettle had done so. He was afraid that Grandpa's curiosity, or the curiosity of others he had told about the grave, might lead them to open it to check things out."[13]

Apparently neither John Zettle nor any other locals who had heard about the fresh dirt on the mountain grave were ever interested enough to investigate the reasons for the curious circumstance. As far as anyone knows, the gravesite remains undisturbed to this day, and the mystery of

---

13. Bill Boswell (born 1920), recorded August 25, 1996.

the missing drover would have remained unsolved, except for the deathbed confession of the man who killed him.

As far as the man who confessed to the murder, "His guilt went with him to his grave," noted John Zettle's grandson. "Nothing could be done to bring the murdered man back," he continued, and those who finally knew the solution to the mystery concluded that had the story become known it would have caused nothing but worry, grief, and shame to the murderer's family."[14]

As a result of the decision to remain silent by those who had heard the dying confession of the man who murdered the drover at the Potters Mills Hotel, the story of the event went into a hibernation of sorts until it was recalled to me by the man who still remembered the tale his mother had told to him.

It's strange how this old tale has resurfaced again after all these years, especially since it seemed to have been put to rest once and for all with the death of the murderer. As a result, if the story itself has not drifted into oblivion, then it doesn't seem too much of a stretch to believe that the spirit of the murdered drover has not yet done so either.

If, as some believe, violent death leads to restless spirits, then the soul of the young drover, just like the story of his death, may not have gone peacefully into eternal rest never to be disturbed again. Then, too, there are those who say he will never find peace, not only due to the way he died, but because his grave has been lost and because he is not buried with the one he loved while here on earth. At least the part about the lost grave is true.

"Many, many, years later, when I had my first car, Mom and I ate a pleasant meal at the old hotel," said our storyteller as he concluded his tale of the murdered drover, "and later that day she tried to locate the grave. But progress had straightened, paved, and relocated the road."[15]

It would seem, then, that the drover's final resting-place has been lost forever. Likewise, there are no traces of the Zettle farm visible anymore today either. Nothing now remains of the buildings except for the crumbling remains of an old stone foundation set back in the woods along the road leading back into the wildest parts of the mountains.

It would therefore be safe to conclude that all earthly links to the story have disappeared and, except for the tale in this book, there will be no

14. Ibid.
15. Ibid.

further evidence that can surface in the future. That, however, may be debatable ground to employees who once worked in the Eutaw House and considered it to be one of the most haunted inns in the United States.

The old stone hotel today (2024) is nothing more than an abandoned hollow shell. Nonetheless, it is still likely home to several spirits, the most prominent being the one the hotel's employees referred to as "Edgar's Ghost" (see the author's story entitled "Raven's Knob" in *Volume IV* of his *Pennsylvania Fireside Tales* series for more details). However, there are other spirits that were known to frequent the place as well, and maybe one of them is that of the unfortunate drover.

Perhaps he still remembers the mountain lass who befriended him in the hotel one day, and perhaps he is looking for her to keep the appointment they had agreed upon but which he was prevented from keeping because of his foul murder. There was another young maid who worked at the Eutaw House in 1989 who just might have experienced the presence of the drover's restless spirit, or that of another of the old inn's ghosts.

After a decade of employment at the ancient hostelry, the young lady had seen and heard some strange things, especially on those late nights when she had to close up the place and was only one of several people left in the building.

"Well, that's when they would come out," claimed the former hotel worker, as she related her experiences to me. "It seemed like when it's real peaceful and quiet is when they would come out," she recalled.[16]

Even though she had experienced walking through "cold spots" in different areas of the hotel and had seen and heard doors open and close mysteriously, she still sometimes got the "creeps" over other strange events that occurred while she worked there in the wee hours of the morning.

"I was in the wine cooler one time talkin' to one of my waitresses," explained the former employee. "This is like at midnight, and the restaurant was closed. All at once we heard footsteps that were phenomenal, like a stampede of elephants were coming! You could feel the floor vibrating!"[17]

To this day the young lady can't explain what happened that night. She had heard of the apparitions seen there by others, including the pipe-smoking gentleman in the top coat and top hat who sometimes appears sitting

16. Trish Miller (born 1967), recorded April 24, 1999.
17. Ibid.

cross-legged in a chair in the President's Room. Then, too, she was aware of the lady in white who seems to float up the stairs leading to second story guest rooms but who can only be seen by the reflection she casts in the old antique mirror on the wall at the foot of the stairs.

Despite being with a co-worker one night when the other woman saw the ghostly reflection in the mirror and turned white as a ghost herself, she was not prepared for what happened on that other night in the haunted place when the thunderous footsteps scared her and another co-worker half to death.

Neither woman that night paused to reflect on whether restless spirits or natural events caused the loud sounds they heard, but if the noises were caused by the ghost of the murdered drover in an attempt to gain an audience with the young ladies, his plan failed miserably.

"We won't tell you what we did!" said my storyteller in a sheepish tone of voice. "Two women, in there by themselves, about had a heart attack!"[18]

18. Ibid.

CHAPTER 2

PETER GROVE AND THE REDHEADED INDIAN

Old Tom Wright should have known better. Or perhaps he was either just an unlucky man or an incredibly stupid one. In any case, he didn't use his best judgment one day in 1727 when he got drunk at John Burt's trading post near the mouth of Swatara Creek, Dauphin County. As it turned out, there were several Indians there at the same time who had also imbibed too much rum.

The "firewater loosened their tongues" to the point that they began to annoy both Burt and Wright. Insults began to fly back and forth, which led to flying fists as well. Wright, fearing for his life, fled to a nearby henhouse, but the Indians caught him there. The next morning, he was found lying dead on the floor. A subsequent inquisition into cause of his death reached the sad conclusion that he died as a result of "several blows on his head, neck and temples."[1]

Wright was the first white man killed by Indians in Pennsylvania. It was the first such homicide since William Penn founded the colony in 1681, and, therefore, seemingly an isolated incident, considering it was the first time it had happened in the forty-five years that Indians and Europeans had been interacting with one another in "Penn's Woods." However, the alarming episode turned out to be the start of what has been described as "one of the most thrilling and bloody chapters in American history."[2]

---

1. C. Hale Sipe, *The Indian Wars of Pennsylvania*, 789.
2. C. Hale Sipe, *The Indian Chiefs of Pennsylvania*, introduction.

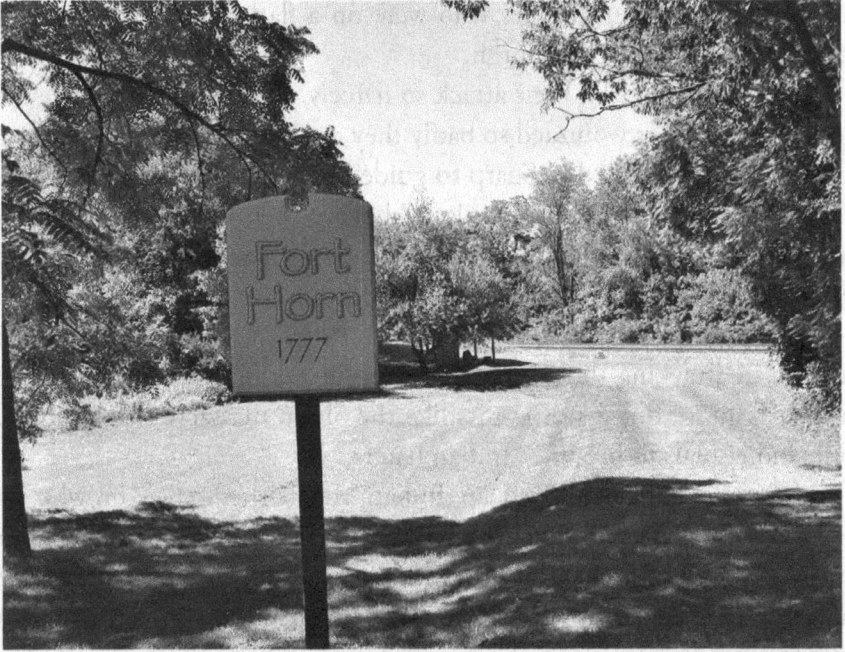

Site of Fort Horn. Located near McElhatten in Clinton County, the sign marks the spot where Samuel Horn, in 1777, stockaded his primitive log home to afford he and his neighbors protection from marauding Indians.

Sporadic slayings of settlers by Indians occurred with increasing frequency after Wright's death, until a wave of terror struck the Pennsylvania frontier in 1755. In July of that year hordes of Indian warriors, emboldened by their defeat of General Braddock's impressive forces in Allegheny County that same month, descended upon pioneer farms and towns.

The German settlements along Penn's Creek, near present day Selinsgrove, Snyder County, were the first to feel the shock of the uprising, but those attacks were quickly followed by others in Fulton, Franklin, Union, Perry, Lehigh, Northampton, Monroe, and other counties. In fact, it would take almost four more decades before the killings finally stopped and the Indians claimed their last victim in Pennsylvania in 1794.

That last incident occurred In May of 1794 when Captain Andrew Sharp, who had been a Revolutionary officer under General Washington, was mortally wounded at the mouth of Two-Mile Run, near present day Apollo in Armstrong County. Here a party of Indians ambushed the Sharp family and two other families who were on a flatboat floating down the Kiskiminetas River to Pittsburgh.

The Indians pressed their attack so fiercely that eventually all the men were either dead or wounded so badly they could no longer steer the boat. It therefore fell upon Mrs. Sharp to guide the craft safely into Pittsburgh, where "the good people of that place," having been warned in advance of the flatboat's approach and the condition of the people on board, "made ready for their comfort and hospitable reception."[3]

Today we can look back and understand why the Indians may have felt justified in attacking those who seemed to be taking over Indian lands in cavalier fashion, but it was events like the Sharp massacre that prompted some individuals to become "Indian haters."

Men who either survived an Indian attack themselves or who had lost loved ones in such attacks sometimes seemed to "snap." Their minds apparently could not rest until they had righted the wrongs that had been inflicted upon them or their families. They in effect dedicated their lives to seeking revenge.

Typical of these eternal foes of the state's native sons were the Walker brothers of Lycoming County. Implicated in the murder of two Indians near Jersey Shore in 1790, the Walkers fled the area and disappeared into the mountains. One of them eventually settled in the mountain wilderness of New York State, where he built a log home. It was unusual to find him there, however, as he preferred a life in the woods, a lifestyle which eventually led his neighbors to refer to him as "the hermit."[4]

Local gossips who claimed to have heard the story from good sources stated that his odd way of living was because of an earlier event in his life that had warped his way of thinking. That event, it was said, although without any certainty, was that both his parents and most of his siblings had been massacred by Indians in Wyoming County, Pennsylvania. He had apparently been captured but had escaped through super-human efforts.

Whatever the truth may be, there is no doubt that he was not a typical frontiersman. He lived in a sort of no-man's land, that boundary between the two conflicting groups where it was sometimes hard to distinguish the settlers' way of life from that of the wilderness life of the Indian. His home

3. Ibid, 543–44.
4. John F. Meginness, *Otzinachson*, 682.

THIS MARKS THE SITE OF
SAMUEL HORN'S FORT
1777
SAID ALSO TO BE THE SITE OF
A MUCH OLDER FRENCH TRADING POST

PLACED BY
THE COLONEL HUGH WHITE CHAPTER
DAUGHTERS OF THE AMERICAN REVOLUTION
1964

THIS MARKS THE SITE OF
SAMUEL HORN'S FORT
1777

Historical marker at Fort Horn. The stone monument marks the exact spot where the historic fort once stood.

territory was, in fact, neutral ground claimed by both parties, where the warring factions would collide, thereby giving both sides an opportunity to display the worst extremes of savagery and cruelty.

The Walkers were not the only inveterate foes of the Indian that came out of the West Branch country of Lycoming and Clinton Counties. That section of the state seems to have produced a disproportionate number of such individuals, but the probability that the development of such men would occur there was probably greater than anywhere else in Pennsylvania.

Warriors of Pennsylvania's Cayuga and Seneca nations had found the Susquehanna's West Branch lands to be one of their best hunting grounds, and when they saw the area being settled by outsiders, the Indians reacted in the only way they knew how. The resulting uprising was only one of many throughout the state during the period of border conflicts that later would give Pennsylvania the distinction of having suffered the bloodiest Indian wars in American history.

It was during the struggle between settlers and Indians over the West Branch territory that several frontiersmen became well known for their prowess as Indian fighters. History has recorded the deeds, both heroic and infamous, of West Branch men like Sam Brady, Moses Van Campen, Robert Covenhoven, Hawkins Boone (a cousin of Daniel Boone), Peter Pence, and others who fought the Indian in the most brutal way, and who often made them pay the ultimate price for their aggression.

The adventures of these fearless borderers are preserved in the historical records of the West Branch, and included in those annals is a firsthand description of Peter Pence which suggests just how tough and rugged he and his compatriots must have been.

According to that account, Pence was most often described by those who knew him personally as "a savage-looking customer," and a man who never went anywhere, even years after peace had settled upon the region, "without being armed with his rifle, tomahawk, and knife."[5]

Although it is Peter Pence's description that has been preserved in the history books, stories of his battles during the Indian wars have not been preserved as much in the oral history of the region as that of another West Branch Indian fighter. Equaling Brady, Van Campen, Pence, and Covenhoven in deeds of daring, Peter Grove's battles with Indians seem to have been the ones that excited people the most and have endured the longest in the folktales of the West Branch Valley.

Said to have been a remarkable sprinter, Grove could outrun any Indian who tried to capture him, and he would often use this athletic prowess to good advantage during surprise attacks he and his frontier compatriots would make on Indian camps. One such attack is still recalled today through the name of Groves Run in Cameron County.

The little stream was so named because it was along here one night that Grove and some fellow rangers made an attack on a number of sleeping

---

5. John Blair Linn, *History of Centre and Clinton Counties*, 605.

Indians, killing them all. There were many other accounts of similar exploits made by this rough frontiersman, and his contemporaries were said to consider his deeds to be equal to that of Captain Jack, the legendary Indian fighter of the Juniata Valley.

As Grove's reputation increased among this own people, he also became well known and feared by his enemies. By the time he had hung up his musket and buried his hatchet, this Holland Dutchman had killed many great warriors. Among his victims were several Indians who were leaders in the fight against the invaders, including the Panther, Greatshot, Blacksnake, and the Wamp.

As a result, Grove became an enemy who was not only feared by the Indians, but who was also a marked man. The only thing, they believed, that would quiet the restless souls of their warrior brothers who had been murdered by Grove would be for them to kill the man themselves.

Historical accounts indicate that Indians of those days were not unlike Europeans when it came to feeling a need to exact revenge upon the murderer of a tribal or family member. On both sides of the conflict there were those who were so doggedly unforgiving that they were driven to seek out and kill someone who had, even years earlier, killed a friend or relative.

Perhaps it was an Indian like this who one day was thwarted in his singular attempt to murder Peter Grove. It is an incident that appears to have escaped inclusion into the historical records of those times, but which has been preserved in the oral history of Clinton County.

The story of this unusual episode was imparted to me one summer afternoon by a white-haired octogenarian while we sat on the front porch of her cabin perched high upon one of the peaks of the Bald Eagle Mountains. The spot afforded a wonderful view of the West Branch Valley below, and the vista extended all the way to Williamsport and the rest of the West Branch country to the east. It was in that very land below that Peter Grove once roamed, and it was here where the unusual story our hostess was about to tell us unfolded.

"My father used to tell us lots of stories about Peter Grove the Indian fighter," said the lady whose ancestors had long called the West Branch Valley their home. "The only one I can remember anymore was the one about the redheaded Indian," she went on, apologizing for her inability to recall any of the other thrilling stories of the pioneer days.

Distant view of Shikellamy's Face along the West Branch. Taken from Blue Hill, Shikellamy State Park, Union County; see chapter 9 in this volume for more details about the Indian face that can still be seen at this site.

"Indians used to camp on the Great Island, but the story my father told was supposed to have happened where Lock Haven State Teachers College is today (since the time of my interview with the lady, Lock Haven State Teachers College has become Commonwealth University—Lock Haven). Here, according to what my father told me, an Indian hid in ambush hoping to kill Peter Grove. The unusual thing about it was that the Indian had red hair."

Maybe Grove spotted the Indian's red hair that day, and maybe that's what saved his life, if the tale is a true one, but the story concludes by noting that Grove was somehow warned in enough time to pull up his musket and shoot the Indian before he could make an attempt on Grove's life. True or not, the account was popular enough to have survived down to the present day and, says the tale, the event was unusual enough to have impressed Peter Grove. It was said he would always tell the story, when recalling his days of the Indian wars, because the Indian "was the only redheaded one that he ever saw!"[6]

---

6. Mila Orner (born 1900), recorded April 21, 1973.

As far as the places and events mentioned in the story of Peter Grove and the redheaded Indian, it can be said that the Great Island mentioned by our storyteller was an important spot for Indian councils. Three of the most important Indian towns in present-day Clinton County were located on or near this Susquehanna River island that sits in the West Branch near the present-day town of Lock Haven. This area of Clinton County was once home to the Wolf clan of Delaware Indians. Known also as the Minsi or Munsee Indians, they were considered to be fierce warriors by those who had ever made the mistake of fighting against them.

So, the location where the redheaded Indian was said to have tried to ambush Peter Grove was certainly in the heart of Clinton County's stiffest Indian resistance, but more will be said about that later. For now, it is interesting to quote a historical account which is strikingly similar to the tale of the redheaded Indian.

"According to tradition," so begins John Blair Linn in his *History of Centre and Clinton Counties, Pennsylvania*, "Peter Grove resided after the war within the bounds of what is now Liberty Township. One day an Indian appeared in the neighborhood where Eagleville now is, and made inquiries respecting the whereabouts of Grove, and was told where he could be found. His informant, upon second thought, concluded the Indian's presence boded no good for Grove, as the former was armed. He immediately hastened to the mill and told Grove what had occurred. The latter took it in a matter-of-fact way, merely remarking that he had no fear of being harmed until sundown.

"Towards the close of the day Grove quit his labors at his water-powered sawmill and proceeded to his cabin to procure his rifle and some old clothes. With the latter he made a dummy, and placing it in position before the mill's saw, started the latter in a slow motion, and retired beneath the banks of the neighboring creek to await developments. The Indian was soon seen stealthily approaching, and upon gaining a favorable position fired his gun at what he supposed was his living enemy. The report had hardly died away when he fell dead, with his brain pierced with a bullet from Grove's rifle. The spot where the Indian is supposed to have been buried is still pointed out to the curious."[7]

Perhaps the stories of the red-headed Indian and the story of an attempt on Grove's life at Eagleville became entwined over time, so that it's no longer

7. John Blair Linn, *History of Centre and Clinton Counties*, 337.

possible to decide how much is fact and how much is fancy. What can be said with assurance today, however, is that the site where the ambush by the red-headed Indian is said to have occurred is on what was the homestead of Cleary Campbell, the first known settler in Clinton County. That land is now part of the campus of Lock Haven State University.

The large island sitting in the West Branch next to Lock Haven is still known as the Great Island today, but the Indians who once lived there were forced out in 1763 by Colonel John Armstrong and a force of three hundred militiamen from Bedford and Cumberland Counties. Five years after that there were a few Shawanese and Delaware stragglers who were living on the Island, including Shawana Ben and Newhaleeka, their chiefs.

Newhaleeka, who was recognized as owner of the island, was one day greatly attracted to a gun and matching equipment owned by William Dunn, a member of a surveying party that had come to the region. After much drinking and some unfair negotiations, Newhaleeka was persuaded by Dunn to trade his island in return for Dunn's armaments and a keg of whiskey. Newhaleeka, after he sobered up, tried to get his island back, but Dunn held the old chief to his original bargain.

Although this account of how William Dunn acquired the Great Island is an unsubstantiated one, the fact that Newhaleeka apparently sold the island to Dunn did not deter the Indians from holding a special place for it in their hearts. For decades afterwards they would return to it, either in person or in their memories. One of the last of his tribe to visit the island was William Dowdy, an Indian of the old "Seneca stock."

He came here, it is said, in 1878, and "lingered for some time," soaking up the charm of the place and the memories of his ancestors it may still have held. It had been his tribe's favorite hunting lands and the place where they had lived, and, he noted, "the cherished spot that contained the bones of his ancestors."[8]

Peter Grove's fate was not a kind one either. Sometime in 1802 or 1803 he and several companions, all of whom had been drinking heavily, were returning from a shooting match. The men were in a canoe, and the river was swollen from heavy rains. Somehow, perhaps through horseplay or an underestimation of the force of the current, the canoe upset.

---

8. John F. Meginness, *Otzinachson*, 83.

View of the Lock Haven University Campus. Perhaps it was at this very spot where Peter Grove was ambushed by the red-headed Indian.

Two of the three men got to shore safely, but Grove floundered and pleaded for help. The men on shore, too drunk to think clearly, thought his cries were attempts to frighten them and watched as Grove sank into the river and drowned. The body of the frontiersman who had cheated death so many times was laid to rest in the Dunnstown Cemetery.

No headstone was set to mark his grave, and for years a large oak tree served as his headstone. The fact that no marker or tombstone was ever erected over the grave of one of the bravest frontiersmen of those times would have pleased his Indian enemies. They may have felt that, in some small way, revenge was theirs at last and the souls of their ancestors could finally rest in peace. Or perhaps they felt that it was the souls of their ancestors that had somehow exacted their own revenge. You see, by a strange twist of fate, the place where Grove drowned was in the river near Dunnstown, just about a mile above the Great Island.[9]

---

9. Ibid.

CHAPTER 3

WHAT'S IN A NAME?

It's certainly not surprising that Pennsylvania's colorful place names have been a subject of interest to many people over the years. The small towns, valleys, mountains, and streams of the Keystone State have been assigned appellations that seem purposely designed to stimulate the imaginations of even the most apathetic individuals.

Both scholars and non-academics, smitten by the romantic images conjured up by Pennsylvania place names such as Aitch, Whiskerville, Fortuneteller Run, Puzzletown, Fools Creek, Devil Alex Hollow, Naked Mountain, and Scalp Level, and many others just as intriguing, have written articles and books on the origins of the more well-known locations.

A. Howry Espenshade's *Pennsylvania Place Names* or Doctor George P. Donehoo's *Indian Place Names In Pennsylvania* are two of the noted classics in the field, but even these two compilations don't include some of the more fascinating place names found in the state. Both of these works do explain the origins of the names of our larger towns, rivers, valleys, and mountain ranges, and in some cases, mention is made of a few of the more entertaining titles of our smaller towns.

However, left out are many other small towns, insignificant streams, isolated villages, or infrequently visited mountains with names that are just as fascinating: names like Deadman's Run, Shy Beaver, Burning Well, Water Plug, White Deer Valley, and Black Log Mountain.

Scholars seem to avoid having anything to do with these smaller places because the origins of their names, in the majority of cases, are preserved

Dinosaur Rock, Lebanon County. Located in the State Game Lands near Mount Gretna, the name of this interesting natural wonder is a lure for hikers and weekend tourists. It's just another example of how curious Pennsylvania place names do indeed have some real thing, person, or event from which they are derived.

only in the cloud-covered realms of oral history and folklore. Nonetheless, there is always a reason for a certain name being chosen for a particular spot.

Most of the time the reason is a commonplace one, such as when a town or valley was named after the first family who settled there, or a mountain was named in honor of a well-known or highly respected individual. Similarly, there are cases where a particular geographic landmark or other feature of the area was the motivation for a name. In yet other cases some thrilling or memorable incident has influenced the choice, but it can be safely said that in all cases there is always a story behind the designations.

Sometimes the story of a place name's origins disappoints the one who is interested enough to find out about it. The tale may reduce a romantic-sounding title, and all the images it evokes, to the commonplace; or just confirm what we had already guessed its origin to be. Although the discovery of the roots of the name can indeed spoil someone's preconceived thoughts about it, the findings may, on the other hand, have the opposite effect. Discovering the roots of a name could, in some cases, cause us to enjoy, or have a greater affinity for, a particular spot; make us feel that we have somehow gotten a little closer to the past.

It's all these possible outcomes, however, that make research into sources of place names not only a time-consuming pastime, but an interesting one as well. Uncovering or hearing a record of a little-known incident that caused an area to be given a particular name is, to the student of such things, a little like finding a gold nugget in a mud bank or a diamond in a coal bin.

One of the reasons that there are so many unusual place names throughout Pennsylvania, and the entire United States for that matter, is because towns big enough to warrant their own post office often had a tough time coming up with a name acceptable to the United States Postal Service. The Post Office Department never liked their post offices to have identical names, and so has always rejected many proposed names that were already in use elsewhere in the United States.

Citizens of a town applying for their own post office would often submit a whole series of fine-sounding names for it, only to have them all rejected. After one choice after another was turned down, the town's naming committee would have to become inventive in order to create a designation acceptable to postal authorities.

That was exactly the dilemma that confronted the people in a small town of Somerset County who were unable to come up with a title agreeable to Uncle Sam in Washington. Exasperated and flummoxed, the townspeople finally threw up their hands. "You name us" was the message they supposedly sent to postal authorities, and that's exactly what the authorities did.[1]

It should be noted, however, that this explanation is a popular tradition without any historical basis and that the Post Office could have chosen that name based upon the name of an original local Indian tribe, the Unami, one of the three sub-tribes of the Lenape or Delaware Indians.

1. John Lichty Jr., "Unamis" *Casselman Chronicle, 1987, Vols. 1, 2,* Springs Historical Society of the Casselman Valley, Somerset County.

Like many other small towns in Pennsylvania, Unamis is not a name that usually can be found on a Pennsylvania road map; the town is too small for that. However, it undoubtedly amuses and intrigues anyone who does look at an index of a Pennsylvania road map and is surprised to find many other names just as quaint or seeing some that are diametrically opposed to others.

The oddities, similarities, and opposites seem like a patchwork quilt sewn together with threads of legends, folk history, local lore, and tall tales. There are so many such opposites, in fact, that this chapter would not be complete without mentioning a few of them (some of the towns that are mentioned in the following paragraphs may no longer exist or their names may have changed over the years, but these little hamlets did actually exist at one time in the counties mentioned and were known by the names given).

It's fun to imagine, for example, what the residents of Drab in Blair County would do if they ever got tired of the scenery there. Would they migrate to Beautiful in Franklin County?

In Columbia or Pike County people living in Stillwater might fancy Cataract in Clearfield or Swiftwater in Monroe.

If you live in Basket in Berks County, you might instead prefer living in Tub in Somerset or High House in Fayette.

If the heights of Summit in Fayette or Cambria Counties, Mountainhouse in Monroe, or Lofty in Schuylkill bother you, try Plains in Luzerne or Ravine in Schuylkill.

Likewise, if Sunnyburn (York County) gets to be too much, you can always move to Shady Plain in Armstrong County or Shadeland in Crawford.

Residents of Panic in Jefferson County might want to consider Fearnot in Schuylkill County or Brave in Greene County.

Then, too, if you're homesick and living in Distant in Armstrong County, why not try Homecamp in Clearfield County, Home in Indiana County, Homewood in Beaver County or Hometown in Schuylkill County?

Scientists have choices as well. If you are a physicist or a chemist you might prefer to live in Laboratory in Washington County, Experiment in Allegheny County, Gravity in Wayne County, or Energy in Lawrence County.

Astronomers will most likely be attracted to Moon Run (Allegheny County), Mars (Butler), Seven Stars (Adams, Huntingdon, Juniata), Telescope (Potter), or Eclipse (Venango).

If you Needmore (Fulton County) or if you're feeling Needful (Clearfield), you might want to seek your fortune and try your luck in Diamond

Scene along the Kildoo Trail. Slippery Rock Creek splashes over the rocks near McConnell's Mills State Park in Butler County.

(Venango County), Pearl (Venango), Gem (Fulton), Bullion (Venango), Jewel (Crawford) or Gold Mine (Lebanon County). However, steer clear of Dearth (Fayette County) and don't live along Poorhouse Run (Huntingdon County).

Those who like a slower pace should consider living in Pokeytown (Somerset County), but if towns and crowds bother you then Sticks (York County) might just be your cup of tea. If, on the other hand, you are a bit depressed, then be sure you don't decide to live near Lamentation Run (Forest County).

Joggers may be delighted to know that there are places in Jefferson County (Big Run or Marathon) or York County (Relay) that might welcome them with open arms. One place they probably will want to avoid, however, is Ache Junction in Fayette County.

There does indeed seem to be a place for almost all types. Even men with beards appear to have a choice (Hairy Spring Hollow in Cumberland County or Whiskerville in Butler County to name just two), as do magicians, who might like Presto (Allegheny County), Magic (Butler), Alladin (Armstrong), Eureka (Montgomery), or Fortune Teller Creek (Fulton).

Whichever town or locale may appeal the most to you, there most likely will still be a question about its name. How did it get that title? What was the source for that odd name? Following are a few of the places that have some of the oddest names in the state, and with them is the purported basis for the names. Readers can decide for themselves whether the explanations are based on fact or not.

ACADEMIA (Juniata County): Tuscarora Academy was founded here in 1836 by Rev. McKnight Williamson, and the school was the basis for the name of the town.[2]

ALFARATA (Mifflin County): Named for a legendary Indian girl of the area. "Wild roves an Indian Girl—Bright Alfarata" was the first stanza of a once-popular folksong that told of the Indian maid who roamed "where sweep the waters of the blue Juniata."[3]

AQUEDUCT (Perry County): Pennsylvania's Main Line Canal System included the Juniata Division, which officially began near Amity Hall. The Division's No. 1 aqueduct crossed the Juniata River here. The aqueduct

2. Frederic A. Godcharles, *Pennsylvania: Political, Governmental, Military and Civil,* 235.
3. Grant N. Sassaman, ed., *Pennsylvania, A Guide to the Keystone State,* 500.

itself, nothing more than a wooden trough with a roof over it, is no longer there. However, its memory is preserved in the name of the small village that grew up around it, and by some of the aqueduct's stone supports that can still be seen here today.[4]

BASKET (Berks County): According to one old-time resident of the county, the town was named after its primary industry: Beaver Basket Works.[5]

BIG SHANTY (McKean County): Named for a large boarding house that once stood by the railroad tracks and was used by railroad workers.[6]

BLACK HOLE VALLEY (Lycoming County): There are two traditions that claim to be the explanation for this particular valley in Clinton Township of Lycoming County, but the following is believed to be the true one. It is related that sometime when this part of Pennsylvania was first being explored and opened up to settlement, a party of prospectors wandered into a swamp that once lay here at the base of the Bald Eagle Mountains. The prospecting party supposedly became mired in the morass, but finally, after much difficulty, extricated themselves. Grateful to be free of the swamp's dark black mud, the exhausted explorers vowed never to be "caught in that black hole again." It was this incident that supposedly led to the name of the valley.[7]

BLACK LOG MOUNTAIN (Huntingdon County): So named from a charred log that was at a favorite stopping place for those passing through a gap in the mountain at this spot. Over the years so many people paused to refresh themselves and to build a fire at various spots around the log that it eventually became charred all over. When others would ask where they had stopped on their journey travelers would answer "at the black log." The name stuck, and was not only eventually applied to the mountain, but also to the valley and stream in this same locale.[8]

BLANKET HILL (Armstrong County): It was from this spot that Colonel John Armstrong and a force of 300 soldiers from Fort Shirley in Cumberland County departed to raid the Indian town of Kittanning in September of 1756. Armstrong left a detachment of thirteen men on the

---

4. Ralph Kinter (born 1915), recorded June 6, 1989; William H. Shank, *The Amazing Pennsylvania Canals*, 19.

5. L. W. Bumbaugh (born 1910), interviewed August 27, 1972, recorded August 22, 1989.

6. McKean County Historical Society, Letter sent to the author, March 13, 1987.

7. John F. Meginness, *Otzinachson*, 669–71; *History of Lycoming County, Pennsylvania*, 581.

8. J. Simpson Africa, *History of Huntingdon and Blair Counties, Pennsylvania*, 341.

hill to watch over a nearby Indian encampment, and he also had all his troops leave their blankets on the hill as well. After Armstrong's departure, the remaining force engaged the nearby Indians in battle, and each and every man was killed. To this day the summit is known as Blanket Hill because the blankets were all that was left of his rear guard when Armstrong returned from his victory.[9]

BLOWVILLE (Potter County): According to some sources this little hamlet was named after a pair of local "blowhards," George and Jolly Carwine, "who were always telling fantastic stories about what they had done around here."[10]

BLUE SHERIFF RUN (Forest County): Tradition states that when the man hired to survey this part of the state was on his surveying expedition, he was accompanied by both the sheriff of Forest County and the sheriff of Warren County. One of the lawmen happened to be dressed in a blue suit, the other in a lighter summer-weight suit. The two small streams that run parallel to each other and flow into Tionesta Creek at this spot had not yet been named, and the surveyor, who was a bit of a humorist, suggested that they be called Blue Sheriff and White Sheriff Runs. Today the little creeks are known by the names of Upper Sheriff Run and Lower Sheriff Run. The small village of Sheriff can also be found near the mouths of the two streams.[11]

BOILING SPRINGS (Cumberland County): Named for a large lake here that is fed by numerous springs from underground caves beneath the lake. The springs bubble up with such force that the waters of the lake appear to be boiling.[12]

BRANDY CAMP (Elk County): Around 1812 William Kersey was hired to survey 145,000 acres of land in this vicinity owned by Fox, Norris and Co. He was also engaged to build a road through the forest in order to open the area up for settlement. Kersey had a crew of men and would build shanties to house them wherever they were working. One such complex was built at present-day Brandy Camp. The name for the little development came about from the fact that Kersey had some choice brandy with him that he would never share with his crew. One day when

9. Grant N. Sassaman, ed., *Pennsylvania, A Guide to the Keystone State*, 402.

10. Potter County Historical Society authors, *Historical Sketches of Potter County*, 226.

11. John T. Faris, *Seeing Pennsylvania*, 298–99.

12. Richard L. Tritt, "Boiling Springs," Cumberland County Historical Society newsletter, winter 1988.

he was out checking on his other camps, his cabin burned down. When the tired surveyor returned, he was shocked to see the charred remains of his house. Upon asking his men what happened, they claimed that local Indians had found his brandy, and, after drinking it all, they then, in their drunken revels, burned down the cabin. Knowing that he couldn't prove that his own men were the ones that had drunk his brandy, Kersey could only accept their story. And to this day the little creek here and the small community that grew up where William Kersey's cabin once stood is still known as Brandy Camp.[13]

CASHTOWN (Adams County): Named from the business practice of one of the settlement's early merchants. Peter Mark, it is recalled, had anything you might want for sale in his store, but insisted that you had to pay cash for it.[14]

COLVER (Cambria County): Derived from the last names of the two gentlemen who promoted the coal business in the area. The person who came up with the name must have been a wordsmith of sorts since he took the first three letters of Mr. Coleman's name and the last three of Mr. Weaver's to form the name of the town. It must have been the same person who also developed the name of the nearby town of REVLOC (a reverse anagram of COLVER).[15]

COON HUNTER (Snyder County): Named from the prevalence of the many hunters who killed raccoons there in the early days.[16]

COUPON (Cambria County): Coal miners here were not paid in cash for their labors. Instead, they were paid in company store coupons which were only redeemable at the store. The name of the town that grew up here from the small mining patch preserves the memory of the much-hated coupons.[17]

CROSS FORK (Potter County): Takes its name from Cross Fork Creek, which was so named by early settlers because of the way the fast-flowing creek crossed over the slower flowing Kettle Creek and "rammed against the opposite bank."[18]

13. W. J. McKnight, *Pioneer Outline History of Northwestern Pennsylvania*, 684.
14. Jacob S. Sheads (born 1910), recorded July 28, 1989.
15. George Korson, *Pennsylvania Songs and Legends*, 314.
16. Snyder County Historical Society, Letter sent to the author.
17. Cambria County Historical Society, Letter sent to the author, June 30, 1985.
18. Robert R. Lyman Sr., *Amazing Indeed*, 27.

CYCLONE (McKean County): Named for a memorable storm that occurred here sometime before 1890.[19]

DEAD WOMAN HOLLOW (Cumberland County): Located in the beautiful South Mountains country near Caledonia State Park, the hollow was named for an unidentified female hiker whose body was found here during the logging era (late 1800s).[20]

DESERTERS RUN (Sullivan County): During the Civil War there occurred numerous "Rebellions in the North," protests and organized revolts by those opposed to the war with the South. Among the most famous was what became known as the Fishing Creek Confederacy. This group of protestors went so far as to build a fort on top of North Mountain in Sullivan County, which served as a refuge for, at most, 50 deserters and draft evaders from Sullivan, Columbia, and Luzerne Counties. Their log blockhouse was built beside a little stream that today is unnamed on Higbee's "Stream Map of Pennsylvania." However older locals still refer to the little creek as Deserters Run, thus preserving the memory of the group of dissidents that considered the place a refuge.[21]

DIAMOND (Venango County): The town was named from the Diamond Inn, an old hotel that once stood on a diamond-shaped piece of real estate in what is still the most northerly village in the county.[22]

DIRTY CAMP (Allegheny County): Said to have been named by Colonel Henry Bouquet's soldiers. His regiments of Highlanders and Royal Americans bivouacked here following a hard-won victory over the Indians at Bushy Run, Westmoreland County, in 1763.[23]

DONATION (Huntingdon County): This little community took its name from a schoolhouse in that neighborhood. The schoolhouse, built in 1833, was erected through the united efforts of the community, whose residents donated their time and money to build it. An old school teacher here suggested the name for the building.[24]

DRIFTWOOD (Cameron County): Its name was borrowed from a creek of the same name, the Driftwood Branch of Sinnemahoning Creek.

19. McKean County Historical Society, Letter to the author, March 13, 1987.
20. Ralph Kinter (born 1915), recorded June 6, 1989.
21. Myrtle Magargel, "The Rebellion in the North," installment 5 in series, *Centre Daily Times*, February 25, 1937.
22. Venango County Historical Society, Letter to the author, August 5, 1986.
23. C. Hale Sipe, *The Indian Wars of Pennsylvania*, 856.
24. J. Simpson Africa, *History of Huntingdon and Blair Counties, Pennsylvania*, 334.

The stream's name was derived from the fact that in earlier days it was much deeper and wider than it is today, and early settlers had to swim their horses to get across. Oftentimes this was not a safe undertaking since flooding was frequent and the raging floodwaters would fill the stream with driftwood—limbs and branches torn from trees and creek-side bushes.[25]

DROMGOLD (Perry County): Residents of this small community in the foothills of the Blue Mountains submitted several names for their post office, but all were rejected until someone suggested that their acting post master submit his name. Thomas Dromgold did just that and it was accepted.[26]

EIGHTY FOUR (Washington County): The name comes from the year 1884, which was the year the post office was established there.[27]

EXPORT (Westmoreland County): Since the coal company in this town was the first in the area to export its "black gold" to outside markets, the townspeople chose that fact as the basis for the name of their post office.[28]

FEARNOT (Schuylkill County): The name for this anthracite town probably has Biblical origins; possibly derived from the 118th Psalm, 6th verse, which reads "The Lord is on my side, I have no fear."[29]

FISHING CREEK (Dauphin County): Supposedly named from the fact that so many bodies were found floating in the creek during the horrible days of the French and Indian War that locals were kept busy fishing out corpses so they could give them a proper burial.[30]

FORTY FORT (Wyoming County): One of the state's frontier strongholds was built on this site in 1770. It was located in a pioneer settlement here that was then known as Forty Town. The name of the town was derived from the forty pioneers who were sent here from Connecticut by the Susquehanna Company to lay claim to the land on behalf of the company. The fort was attacked and captured by the British and their Indian

25. Rosa A. Nelson, "Colorful History of a Clinton County Hunter Pioneer of the 1800s, *Daily Record*, Lock Haven, PA. Provided to the author by Mrs. R. Caskey of Renovo.

26. Gladys Dromgold Schaffer, "Dromgold Corner Remembrances," *Perry County Times*, February 14, 1991.

27. George Swetnam and Helene Smith, *A Guidebook to Historic Western Pennsylvania*, 226.

28. Grant N. Sassaman, ed., Pennsylvania, *A Guide to the Keystone State*, 394.

29. Northumberland County Historical Society, Letter to the author, February 25, 1995.

30. Ralph Kinter (born 1915), recorded June 6, 1989.

allies in 1778, thereby opening up the entire Wyoming Valley to the bloody incursions of Indian war parties.[31]

GREENCASTLE (Franklin County): Laid out in 1782 by Colonel John Allison, the town's name was originally spelled Green-Castle. The name came from Allison's hometown in Ireland, a small seaport in County Donegal on the coast of the Emerald Isle.[32]

HARTS LOG VALLEY (Huntingdon County): Indian trader John Hart set up his trading post where the village of Alexandria now stands sometime prior to 1750. Here he felled a huge white oak tree and cut troughs in it where he would place salt and feed for the horses in his pack train. It was this landmark that led to the name of the valley and to the stream, both of which still bear the name today.[33]

HOME (Indiana County): In 1840 the post office for Kellysburg in Rayne Township was established in the home of Hugh Cannon. The name Kellysburg was probably in use as the name of a post office elsewhere, and so locals decided to use Cannon's "home" as the basis for the name of their village.[34]

HONEY CREEK (Mifflin County): Local legend states that back in the mid to late 1700s James Alexander lived at the head of the little creek that bears the distinction of being the shortest in the United States. "Honey Jim," as he was known to his neighbors, was a farmer, but he also kept 99 hives of bees on his property. The hives were all located on a hilltop near Honey Jim's homestead, but eventually it occurred to him that his bees might have better access to the blossoms of the black locust trees around the spring below if he moved his hives down there. So, one day "Honey Jim" moved all his hives to the lower ground near the spring that is the source of the stream. All went well for a while until heavy rains caused a flash flood. The flood washed all Jim's hives, along with their delicious combs of honey, into the unnamed stream. The event was such a memorable one that the creek was thereafter christened Honey Creek, a name which is still assigned to it yet today.[35]

31. Thomas L. Montgomery, ed., *Frontier Forts of Pennsylvania, Volume I*, 438.
32. Grant N. Sassaman, ed., *Pennsylvania, A Guide to the Keystone State*, 485.
33. Albert Rung, *Rung's Chronicles of Pennsylvania History*, 290; J. Simpson Africa, *History of Huntingdon and Blair Counties, Pennsylvania*, 408.
34. Indiana County Historical Society, Letter to the author, September 11, 1984.
35. Honey Creek Inn, Reedsville, PA, menu information, September 3, 2001.

HOP BOTTOM (Susquehanna County): Named from Hop Bottom Creek near here. The creek was named after the abundance of wild hops that once grew along its banks. The dried flowers of the hop plant are used to add flavor to beer and ale.[36]

HUNGRY HOLLOW (Potter County): Sometime when this northern country was first being explored, a party of men got stranded in the wilderness. They set up a temporary camp along a little stream that drains into present day Cross Fork Creek. The explorers ran out of food and nearly starved before they got themselves out of their predicament, and to this day the hollow where their camp was located is referred to as Hungry Hollow by locals.[37]

JUG HANDLE CREEK (Forest County): Pioneer hunter Ebenezer Kingsley settled in this section of the state in 1825. He named many of the streams through here based on events that occurred near each one. In this case he decided to call the stream Jug Handle Creek "because it was here, at the mouth of the creek, that he broke the handle off his jug."[38]

NOLO (Indiana County): Located on an elevation that situates it higher than the land around it, the story goes that residents chose this name for their settlement because there is "No Low" ground to be found in the town itself.[39]

NORVELT (Westmoreland County): An anagram formed by the last three letters of Eleanor Roosevelt's first name and the last four of her last name.[40]

PUZZLETOWN (Blair County): The town's unusual name is based on the many legal disputes over land ownership here. The court cases began shortly after the time the village was first laid out in 1840 and continued for many years.[41]

SCALP LEVEL (Cambria County): Local tales indicate that the town was named from an incident that occurred during a "clearing bee" or "frolic" that was held by Jacob Esh, Jr., along Paint Creek in 1794. Esh wanted land cleared along the creek for a sawmill and gristmill he planned to build there, and in order to save money on the project he invited neighbors to

36. Grant N. Sassaman, ed., *Pennsylvania, A Guide to the Keystone State*, 474.
37. Robert R. Lyman Sr., Amazing Indeed, Strange Events in the Black *Forest*, 43.
38. William J. McKnight, *Pioneer Outline History of Northwestern Pennsylvania*, 527.
39. Sassaman, Ibid, 401.
40. Ibid, 571.
41. Tarring S. Davis, *A History of Blair County, Pennsylvania, Volume I*, 113.

clear the land, with the promise of drinks "on the house." After passing around a jug of moonshine, Jake then supposedly got everyone working with the cry of "Scalp 'em level boys!" The event was a success, and when it came time to pick a title for the town, Jake Esh's words were remembered and adopted by locals as the name they liked the best for their community.[42]

SHY BEAVER (Huntingdon County): Named for the creek of the same name that enters Raystown Lake at this point. Early settlers gave the creek this unusual name because even though they could see plenty of evidence of beavers being active in the creek, they could never see them.[43]

SLIPPERY ROCK (Butler County): This unusual name comes from nearby Slippery Rock Creek. The creek was named from a large rock lying on the east bank about six miles south of the site of the old gristmill built by Daniel Kennedy in 1868. It is thought that it was here, near a shelf of sandstone, that an Indian trail (perhaps a branch of the Logstown Path or the Kuskusky-Venango Path) forded the stream. A natural oil seep made one large rock at the ford exceptionally slick, and it was this landmark that was the basis for the name of the creek. Although the rock is still here, near present-day Armstrong Bridge in McConnell's Mill State Park, the oil that once seeped from the ground was drained away by oil wells that flourished here in the late 1800s.[44]

TELESCOPE (Potter County): "This was a station on the B & S railroad about Kilbourne or West Pike. Here a new factory was built in the early 1900s that made cot beds that folded, hence the name Telescope."[45]

TURNUP RUN (McKean County): Located near the present-day village of Westline, the creek was a landmark for travelers in the late 1800s. It was said that when traveling to Glen Charles, an old lumber town in the Black Forest, you made your way along Kinzua Creek until you got to Turnup Run, where you "turned up" to go north to Glen Charles. The name has been sometimes corrupted and spelled as Turnip Run.[46]

TURKEY FOOT (Franklin County): South of Chambersburg, where Route 995 and Township Road 3012 meet, sits the small Franklin County

42. Cambria County Historical Society, Letter to the author, June 30, 1985.
43. Gladys Grubb, "What's in a Name?" Raystown Project, Huntingdon County Historical Society, post-1977; Letter to the author December 07, 2005.
44. Pennsylvania Department of Conservation and Natural Resources, "McConnells Mill State Park," 5. Dcnr.state.pa.us/stateparks/parks/McConnellsmill.aspx.
45. Potter County Historical Society authors, *Historical Sketches of Potter County*, 224.
46. McKean County Historical Society, Letter to the author, March 13, 1987.

town with this unusual name. The name comes from the shape of the road junction, which resembles the imprint of a wild turkey's foot.[47]

VINCO (Cambria County): It is recalled that there were many men who lived here that liked to chew tobacco, and supposedly the town was named from their favorite brand of chewing tobacco.[48]

WATER PLUG (Perry County): Now only a cluster of two homes, this place was once the site of a railroad water tower. Trains would stop at the tower to take on water and to pick up farmers' produce. The original railroad bed can still be seen today, but the tower is gone.[49]

WEIGH SCALES (Northumberland County): One of a number of coal patches in this and surrounding counties, the town's name no doubt came from the odd nomenclature of the anthracite mining industry that was once the predominant employer here.[50]

WIDOW SPRINGS (Franklin County): Legends here claim that at this site in the foothills of the Blue Mountains northwest of Shippensburg, locals found the body of a woman who was thought to be the widow of a man who was killed for his winnings by fellow gamblers in Dillsburg. Some legendary accounts state that she tracked down and killed three of the murderers, before stopping to camp at the springs. Here the fourth gambler, realizing she was on his trail, found her and murdered her before she could do the same to him![51]

WILD BOY RUN (Potter County): A stream named for Lewis Stevens, an unusual hermit who settled in this remote part of Potter County in 1842. He built himself a log hut and lived a solitary life, surviving by eating wild berries and nuts, and by hunting and fishing. It isn't exactly clear today why his neighbors referred to Stevens as "the wild boy." Perhaps it was because he was a hermit and seemed to shun the company of others. However, in reality he probably wasn't any wilder than his neighbors, all of whom were fiercely independent and rugged mountaineer types who preferred to live in the wilderness rather than suffer in the confined spaces of a city.[52]

---

47. Jim Stephens (born 1924), recorded December 23, 1989.
48. Cambria County Historical Society, Letter to the author, June 30, 1985.
49. Mrs. James Ettien, Water Plug, interviewed May 1985.
50. Grant N. Sassaman, ed., *Pennsylvania, A Guide to the Keystone State*, 536.
51. Michael P. Henson, *A Guide to Treasure in Pennsylvania*, 27.
52. Elmer L. Smith, ed., *Logging in the Pennsylvania North Woods*, 35.

WILMERDING (Allegheny County): Named for Joanna Wilmerding Negley, the highly respected wife of William B. Negley, a large landholder in the area.[53]

WINTERBURN (Clearfield County): Some authorities think this small hamlet was named after a village in Scotland, but there are others who say that the name comes from the fact that the clearing for the first settler's log cabin here was "burned" off in the wintertime.[54]

ZELIENOPLE (Butler County): Surely an unusual place name in anyone's opinion, but an even stranger cognomen for a person. Nonetheless, the name for this place was chosen by Baron Dettmar Basse, the founder of the town. He was devoted to his beloved daughter, whose nickname was Zelie, but for some reason was also an admirer of the Turkish city of Constantinople. He combined the two names when choosing a name for his village.[55]

By now it should be obvious that Pennsylvania has a town with a name designed to please almost anyone. There are many other highly unusual place names in Pennsylvania that could have been included in this chapter, but it is nonetheless a fact that despite the delightful variety of choices available to us, there will always be some people who may not ever find any place here in the Keystone State that appeals to them in any way. In those cases, the dissatisfied seeker might still consider Content (Jefferson County) or, better yet, Hearts Content (Warren County), as likely alternatives.

---

53. Wilmerding website, internet, January 12, 2004.
54. Lewis Cass Aldrich, *History of Clearfield County, Pennsylvania*, 561.
55. Grant N. Sassaman, ed. *Pennsylvania, A Guide to the Keystone State*, 590; and details, Potter County Historical Society letter to the author, July 13, 1990.

CHAPTER 4

EYE TO EYE WITH DEATH

In the eleventh chapter of the author's previous volume in this series there are a number of stories that are best classified as tall tales. They are labeled as such, and the chapter in which they are included is appropriately titled "Stretching It," because the anecdotes were obviously created to amuse the listener by stretching the truth way past the breaking point.

These types of tales certainly did not originate in Pennsylvania, nor can it be said that they are solely an invention of Americans. When and where this style of storytelling originated is a point best left to scholars of such things, but there seems to be little doubt that one of the best-known raconteurs of the tall tale was Baron Karl Friedrich von Munchausen.

The Baron of Tall Tales, as he was to become known throughout the world, first became famous around Hanover Germany in the 1760s. The baron's extraordinary recollections of his adventures as a hunter, sportsman, and soldier in the Russian wars with the Turks, were so fantastic and so entertaining that they caught the fancy of everyone who heard them. Eventually his anecdotes were published in several languages and became popular wherever they were read.

Munchausen was so adept at telling his fictions with a straight face, a characteristic of any good teller of tall tales, that many people believed he was actually telling the truth. As I've said before in several of my previous volumes, one of the characteristics of a good storyteller is that he is able to stretch the truth in a way that it's not always obvious to the listener that he's doing so.

There were many individuals with such talents here in Pennsylvania in the old days when the main form of entertainment was storytelling, and so the reader may think that the following tale is just an entertaining creation from the mind of my informant. In fact, upon reading the tale, there are many who will undoubtedly categorize its teller as a raconteur whose talents for exaggeration match those of the famous von Munchausen himself. The setting of the story is wintertime, on Big Poe Mountain in Centre County, around 1917.

"I was living on my own farm near Zerby Station at that time," began Ralph Lingle, lifelong mountain man and old-time hunter. "One morning I was driving my team of horses through Poe Valley and found a dead deer lying on the road. It had really been chewed up, but whatever had attacked it hadn't eaten it. Just killed it out of meanness, I guess!

"Later on, Charlie Smith and I found other dead deer in the same shape, as well as grouse and rabbits. It was the same thing with these; whatever killed them never ate any of the game she killed! Well, we figured that this would eventually be hard on the deer herd, so we decided to do something about it.

"So, one clear cold winter morning we set out to hunt this down. It didn't take us long to pick up some big cat tracks in the snow, and we followed them up the mountain. We had to push through waist deep snow, but we soon came to another deer. Near it we could see where the thing that had jumped on it and chewed it up had been hiding. We went over and paced off the distance from its hiding place to where it had landed on the deer. It was twenty good steps!

"We left the deer behind and kept following the tracks, and it wasn't long before we found a grouse with its head eaten off. From here we saw more tracks leading off to a V-shaped ravine to the west, which is the one right below where the fire tower stands today. It was really rocky in there and we could see that the tracks led right into a big opening in the rocks.

"The darn rocks were all frozen together, so we cut down a small tree and used it as a pole to start prying the rocks apart. After a little of that we poked the pole into the hole, and when we pulled it back out there was hair all over the end. I poked my head into the hole to see if I could see anything, and when I did, I saw two eyes as big as flashlights about two feet from my face! We poked our pole back into the hole, but this time the thing in there grabbed onto it, pulled it right out of our hands and all the way into the hole! Charlie wanted me to crawl in and grab onto the pole and pull it back out. I told him I didn't want any part of that, and so we talked about shooting it.

"We figured the thing was a wildcat or something like it and so wanted its fur for the bounty. But we thought if we shot it, we'd damage the fur. I had a .30-30, but Charlie had a 12-gauge shotgun, so we decided to remove some powder from one of his shells and shoot it with that. We loaded the shell into the shotgun and then poked the barrel into the hole until it was probably about two feet from the animal's head.

"We fired off the gun, and then I poked my head down in the hole again, but I saw the same thing. The eyes were still there, glaring out at me. I wasn't about to crawl down there, and neither was Charlie, so we loaded a shell with a full charge into the shotgun and shot into the hole again.

"This time when I looked in, I couldn't see no eyes, so I crawled all the way down in and found a big cat, deader than a doornail! After we pulled it out, we took a good look at it, and were we surprised! It wasn't a wildcat, but was bigger, grayish in color, and it had spots. It was so long that its head dragged on the ground after I slung it over my shoulder and started back down off the mountain. We didn't save its paws or anything as souvenirs, but we did get two dollars bounty for it. Charlie sent the hide off to the Harter Fur Company and they told us it was a Canada lynx." Reflecting a moment, Mr. Lingle, with a hint of regret in his voice and remembering the old hunting days, noted that the unusual feline "was probably one of the last ones shot in these parts!"[1]

At the present time almost no one knows, or would believe, that such an animal as the Canada lynx was once found in the more isolated parts of Pennsylvania's forests. Closely related to other big cats, the eastern Canadian lynx was, says historian W. J. McKnight in writing of the Canada lynx in northwestern Pennsylvania, "often mistaken for a panther."[2]

Although it's a short-tailed cat and not nearly as large as a mountain lion, the Canada lynx is larger than its cousin the wildcat, or eastern bay lynx, and was once a valuable prize for a hunter. The cat's fur was valued

1. Ralph Lingle (born 1900), interviewed August 27, 1972.
2. William J. McKnight, *Pioneer Outline History of Northwestern Pennsylvania*, 119, 130.

The Big Grey Wildcat. This artist's rendition of a Canada
Lynx, once called a "big grey wildcat" by early hunters,
portrays what these wily cats looked like when they shared the
Pennsylvania forests with their mountain lion cousins – drawn
by James J. Frazier

for trimming garments, and due to its elusive ways, the animal was a true challenge for some of the rugged hunters of earlier days. To such men only the panther and the Canada lynx provided sport that was exciting enough for them to go that "extra mile" to bag their trophy.

Today the exploits of these mighty hunters have been all but forgotten by present generations. However, ten to fifteen years ago there were still old-timers who were happy to relate tales of some of the exciting hunting episodes that were told to them when they were young. These were accounts they had heard from the mouths of old men who knew the celebrated nimrods of their earlier days and who loved to tell and retell their stories about them. Very few individuals like that are around today, but fourteen years ago there was at least one man who could still recall the old accounts of the chase, and one of his recollections alluded to the presence of the lynx in the isolated parts of the Blue Mountains of Dauphin County in earlier days.

"When I was a kid, Ike Strawl told me he used to run a lot of fox hounds," said eighty-two-year-old Jack Strawl. The old man was living with his wife, in the family homestead along the foot of Short Mountain in Clarks Valley, when I interviewed him in 1991, and he proved to be a good source of entertaining tales of the long ago.

"Ike was ninety-six when he died, but he spent most of his life in the mountains," continued Mr. Strawl. "He was really a mountaineer! He was a great foxhunter, but he told me he used to run 'cattymounts' over here in Fishing Creek. Well, 'cattymount' is French for 'mountain cat', so we must've had a couple around!"[3]

"Cattymount," the term Ike Strawl used to describe the animal his fox hounds used to run, was no doubt a variation of the term catamount. And the term, according to Mr. McKnight in his *Pioneer Outline History of Northwestern Pennsylvania*, published in 1905, was the common name used by hunters in this section of Pennsylvania when referring to the Canada lynx. Likewise Rhoads, in his *Mammals of Pennsylvania and New Jersey*, includes a description of how one Tioga County hunter caught a Canada lynx in his traps "about the time of the War of the Rebellion," and states that here these "larger species of wildcats were called catamounts."[4]

In northern Pennsylvania, hunters once referred to the Canada lynx as the catamount and also as the big grey wildcat,[5] while biologists refer to it in their taxonomy as *Lynx Canadensis*. But despite the uncertainty in how it should be referred to, there seems little doubt that the catamount does have a unique ability to jump long distances in single bounds. For those who want further proof in that regard, an old account from a McKean County hunter may shed some light on that subject.

During the trying times of the Civil War years, Thomas Fenton decided to seek some peace and solitude in the woods near his hunting

3. Jack Strawl (born 1909), recorded April 24, 1991.
4. Samuel N. Rhoads, *Mammals of Pennsylvania and New Jersey*, 139.
5. Henry W. Shoemaker, *Pennsylvania Wild Cats*, 14. (Shoemaker's information is always suspect, and in this case I could find no primary sources that confirmed that "big grey wildcat" was used to refer to the Canada lynx in Pennsylvania or elsewhere.)

camp along Kinzua Creek. He carried his musket with him, hoping to find a nice deer he could shoot for his family larder, and soon his patience and hunting skills were rewarded when a large doe appeared on the other side of the creek. With one shot Fenton brought down the deer. After he had dragged it close to his camp, he dressed it and hung it on a high tree branch. The next evening when he came back to get it, he found that something had come within about ten feet of the tree and then pounced upon the meat in a single leap from that far away. He set a trap for the predator, and when he caught it several days later, he found it to be "a nice specimen of Canadian Lynx."[6]

Using steel traps was probably the easiest way to catch the Canadian lynx or even its cousin the bay lynx. Any other approach had its difficulties, no matter which cat a hunter was trying to bag. Hunters like Ralph Lingle and Charlie Smith found that out when they tried to bring down their Canada lynx, but Huntingdon County trapper and mountain man John P. Swoope found out the same thing when he tried to corral a bay lynx one day.

Swoope's hunting exploits, some once believed, "deserve to be rated with those of Davy Crockett."[7] But of all his adventures, one of his most exciting occurred in November of 1908 when he and some companions were using a pack of dogs to track wild cats on Tussey Mountain. They succeeded in following one set of tracks into Harrys Valley and then over to Round Top Mountain, where they found the dogs had holed up a wild cat in some rocks. Not willing to wait around for the animal to come back out, Swoope decided to go in after it.

"I crawled in to look for it," wrote the old hunter in his diary, "and it ran out over my back, sinking its claws into my hunting coat." Swoope's dogs wasted no time in treeing the fleeing wild cat in a nearby pine tree. With two well-aimed shots, Swoope was able to bring the cat down, thereby ending what he termed "a very hard hunt," and also noting that they had "traveled over ten miles of woods and rocks before getting the animal."[8]

Up in Tioga County there is a similar story told about an unusual devotee of the chase named Step'n'half Razy. Although the old-time hunter was best known for his nom-de-plum, his reputation as a panther hunter was

---

6. Rhoads, Ibid, 137.
7. Ibid.
8. Albert Rung, *Rung's Chronicles of Pennsylvania History*, 214.

Old-time hunter and trapper E. N. Woodcock. (Born in 1844, he often heard the wolves howl and saw their tracks when he went on daily inspections of his many traplines in the Black Forest of Potter County.)

the other thing that people remembered about him. Razy got his unusual name from the fact that, due to a "gimpy" leg, he had an unusual gait. Instead of taking two long strides like most people do when they walk, Razy took a "step and a half" to get where he was going. However, this slow pace didn't seem to prevent him from joining in hunts for local mountain lions.

Razy and his fellow hunters would track a big cat for miles until it tired and holed up in the relative safety of a cave. This strategy didn't discourage Razy, and much to the amazement of his companions, he would crawl into the cave and, without fail, shoot the panther. Probably some of those same caves may yet be found today near the villages of Leetonia and Sabinsville, but Razy's memory still lives on through the local place names of Step'n'half Hollow and Step'n'half Creek.[9]

Clearfield County also can claim a courageous hunter like Step'n'half Razy, and his exploits were just as remarkable. One of the first settlers in that county was Daniel Turner, who settled at the mouth of Clearfield Creek in 1802. Regarded as a "bold, daring, and powerful man," he was best known as a panther hunter, and especially for a "rough and tumble" match he had with one of the beasts. He managed somehow to get hold of its hind legs in such a way that it could not bite or claw him, and he held on until a companion came by and killed the cat with his hatchet.[10]

It is also reported that Turner had yet another close encounter with a mountain lion. In this case he shot the beast, but only winged it. The wounded animal managed to drag itself into a deep crevice between two large rocks, but Turner was not about to let his trophy escape. Fastening a "sword-like bayonet" to the barrel of his musket, the determined hunter crawled into the cave-like fissure and managed to kill the big cat by stabbing it numerous times. It was a feat noteworthy enough to be recorded in the historical annals of the region. To put oneself in such a precarious position requires raw courage and, noted the historian who recorded the event, "Few men would care to tackle a wounded panther in a place like that."[11]

Panthers weren't the only animals that liked to hole up in rocky clefts or in limestone caves when being pursued by a hunter determined to bag a trophy no matter how hard or risky the effort. There are also episodes on record of how wolves would sometimes take refuge in such places in a last desperate effort to elude their human pursuers, only to be surprised to find one of those same pursuers boldly crawling in after them.

Up in Cameron County, near the village of Shippen Station around 1830, William Lewis and Ben Freeman tracked a wolf to its rocky den in what, today, are the Elk State Forest lands. Lewis asked Freeman to remain outside while he crawled into the opening in the rocks. Lewis said he would "hunt him out," and that Freeman was to shoot the animal when it came out of the den.[12]

9. James Y. Glimm, *Flatlanders and Ridgerunners*, 173.
10. Lewis Cass Aldrich, *History of Clearfield County, Pennsylvania*, 56.
11. Ibid.
12. McKnight, Ibid, 488.

Lewis would later relate that at first, he could see nothing in the darkness of the passageway he was crawling through, but then in the black void ahead he could see the glaring eyes of the wolf. Undeterred, the daring hunter continued to crawl toward the wolf in a reckless variation of the game of chicken. Neither prey nor predator seemed likely to back down first, until finally the wolf had had enough. With a violent lunge, the animal jumped past its pursuer and managed to reach the opening to its former hiding place, only to be gunned down by Ben Freeman.

Freeman must have at first wondered what had happened to his companion when he did not directly emerge from the wolf's lair, but eventually Lewis crawled out into the light of day. With him he was carrying two wolf pups he had found when he crawled on back to where the she wolf had made its last stand. Lewis carried the two whelps home with him, where he may have tried to domesticate them.[13]

European traditions also support the claims that hunters sometimes took remarkable risks by crawling into a wolf's lair or panther's den in order to claim a prestigious trophy of the chase. In his fascinating collection of hunting days in early Europe, James Harting, for example, preserves a Scottish tale of how one of the lairds of Chisolm came face to face with a wolf in her den sometime in the sixteenth century.

The wolf in question had settled inside a large cairn in that section of the country known in those days as the Wolves' Glen, or *Gleann Chonfhiadh*. Here, inside the loose pile of rocks, the she-wolf was raising her litter of pups, but at night she was in the habit of emerging from her den and terrorizing the countryside. Over time the animal became so bold that she attacked and killed several people, and her reputation eventually attracted the attention of the young laird and his brother.

The two gallant hunters managed to track the wolf to its den, but when they got there, they discovered by her tracks that she had sallied forth on another hunt. However, they could hear the patter of the young whelps' feet and their cries coming from the den, and that was enough to spur the eldest brother into action.

Taking his dirk in his right hand and his steel gauntlet in the left, the fearless Scotsman crawled into the den and began extracting his vengeance upon the young wolves. While the determined laird was performing his

13. Ibid.

Wolverine in a glass cage. Another ferocious predator that could once be found in our Pennsylvania mountains. (On display in a museum at the University of Michigan.)

bloody work, the mother wolf returned and, maddened by the desperate cries of her pups, rushed into the den. Her attack was so swift that the younger brother, who had been posted outside to guard for such an eventuality, could not react quickly enough to impale her with his spear. His throw went wild and hit a rock instead, breaking the point off the weapon.

Inside the den, the eldest Chisolm managed to reverse his position in time to greet the incoming wolf head on. With a remarkable presence of mind, he thrust his steel-gauntleted hand into the open jaws of the wolf's mouth, and then proceeded to repeatedly stab the animal in its breast until it was dead.[14]

Pennsylvania can claim its own group of hunters whose courage rivaled that of the bold lairds of Chisolm. Up in Jefferson County there is an account preserved of how, sometime in the 1830s, a Mr. Long and two of Frederick Kahle's sons, John and Jacob, trapped eight young wolves in a den along Mill Creek one day. Unwilling to give up the chase, the three men decided that one of them should crawl into the den and try to pull the wolves out.

The account does not say whether the men drew lots for the privilege of crawling into the wolves' den, or whether John, the oldest of the Kahles, volunteered for the job. In any case, the elder Kahle, armed with a torch

14. James E. Harting, *Extinct British Animals*, 173.

light in one hand, and a five-foot-long stick with a hook on the end to catch on to a wolf in the other, made eight entries into the den without snaring a single wolf. Then, on his ninth try, he managed to hook the oldest wolf and tugged on the rope tied around his foot as a signal for the others to pull him out. The wolf proved to be too heavy, however, and the men had to give up.

Mr. Long, though disappointed, was not yet defeated, and offered the elder Kahle ten dollars to make a tenth attempt. When the young man declined, Long took his knife and gun and crawled in after the wolf himself. After a fourth try, the old hunter had to admit defeat himself, because even though he had seen the wolf, he had neither been able to get close enough to stab the beast nor to get positioned well enough to draw a bead on it. On the other hand, he did come away with a story that, although it sounded far-fetched, would never cease to be a source of entertainment for his hunting buddies or for his grandchildren.[15]

Baron Karl Friedrich von Munchausen would have been favorably impressed with the story of the Chisolm brothers and their wolf hunt, just as he would have enjoyed the tales of the Kahle brothers, Ralph Lingle, and others like them. He would have no doubt incorporated a version of the episodes into his own repertoire of tall tales had he known about such daring-do. Had he told such a tale in his own inimical style, however, he would have cast doubts upon the veracity of the Chisolm brothers and other hunters like them, who in reality were bold enough to come "eye to eye with death" in the confines of a wolf's den or panther's lair.

15. William H. Egle, *History of the Commonwealth of Pennsylvania*, 804.

CHAPTER 5

DRIVING IN THE PEG

(And other tales of Pennsylvania Witchcraft)

In my last volume of *Pennsylvania Fireside Tales*, there is a chapter titled "A Witches Brew," and in it are old-time witch tales that I described as "some of the best I've been able to collect over the years." However, I've been told an amazingly large number of original witch stories in my fifty years of traveling through the mountains of Pennsylvania, and I'm left with many that in my mind are just as entertaining as those in *Volume V*. Moreover, these other stories include witchcraft motifs that were never brought to light in *Volume V*'s tales at all; and it seemed to me that these other anecdotes deserve to be preserved as much as the witch episodes in any of my previous volumes in this series. Therefore, this chapter includes more of my favorite tales of hexerei that I've collected in the hills of the Keystone State.

Although I've often touched upon this aspect of the witch genre in previous episodes I've related, the tales in this chapter are concerned more with the measures people thought they should take if they felt they were the target of a witch's spell. It seems that for one reason or another there have been standards of sorts established in the matter of ridding oneself from evil spells cast by an old hex, but there are many variants as well.

Many of these so-called remedies or counterspells are probably as old as the belief in witchcraft itself, but others seem to be new ideas thought up by those who, in more recent times, claimed to be able to use their own supernatural powers to counteract the spells of evil witches. These "good

Gliding across the face of the pale yellow moon. A depiction of how people once believed broomsticks were used by witches in their nocturnal missions to inflict pain and torment upon people as well as animals. (Public domain Illustration from Charles Mann's "In the Heart of Cape Anne, Or the Story of Dogtown" – published in 1906.)

witches," or *brauchers* in the Pennsylvania Dutch idiom, more than likely realized that the more sensational and unique their remedies the more likely it was their reputations would spread.

This first tale, I think, illustrates this point better than most, but some of the other anecdotes that I've included in this chapter do so as well. The following tales also vividly show that in the distant past many people did not consider natural causes to be reasonable explanations behind strange events, turning instead to their beliefs in witchcraft to come up with their own cause-and-effect scenarios.

THE BEWITCHED CORN

The setting for this story, which I collected in 1983, is in Georges Valley of Centre County. It is an excellent example of how a lack of basic scientific knowledge can be exploited. The gentleman who told me the story was a strong believer in the power of witchcraft. When he told me the following tale, he was still convinced that years earlier his corn crop and some corn he and his wife had canned were ruined by an evil spell cast by his neighbor, and that this same spell was broken by a local braucher.

"One year our corn crop got all wormy, so we went and got some corn off a guy and canned it," began the valley farmer and mountain man. "In the meantime, somebody went and stole some corn off a neighbor of ours. This other guy found out we'd canned all this corn and blamed us for stealin' his. Then our corn we'd canned started to spoil, so I went out to see old Ben Ripka one night and told him what was goin' on.

"He told us to make fire in the cook stove and get her good and hot. And he said, 'Just as the clock is striking midnight, throw a quart jar of your canned corn in.' Man, I don't know what Bennie did to that corn, but there was an explosion that blew the griddles off the stove and put the fire out!"

"The next day at work I hear this neighbor of ours tellin' another guy that he had such a headache he thought his head was gonna blow off! That stopped the corn from spoilin'!"[1]

WITCHING OFF HER EARS

The same gentleman who recalled the previous story also related the following episode to me, and his wife confirmed the details. The anecdote once again shows how a lack of understanding about the basic laws of nature can lead some people to attribute marvelous powers to practitioners of both white and black magic.

The setting for this tale is along the Paradise Road near the small village of Greenbriar in Eastern Penn's Valley of Centre County, sometime in the last decades of the nineteenth century. The hex in the story was a woman who, some once believed, got her ears "witched off" because of her penchant for casting evil spells on others. Lena Lingle, the hex woman in this story, was the great-grandmother of my storyteller's wife. The name of the young girl the hex was trying to intimidate was Florence Confer. Many of the older generation who lived around the time the events unfolded, and many of their descendants, considered the story to be a true one. The motivation for the casting of the evil spells was Lena's dissatisfaction with the new gentleman who was keeping company with her friend Florence.

---

1. Ray Rowles (born 1933), recorded July 27, 1983, July 5, 1984, and May 26, 1988.

For some reason Lena felt the young man just wasn't right for her bosom buddy. She must have tried to convince Florence that she should try to find another boyfriend, but her powers of persuasion fell upon deaf ears. It was at that point that Lena decided to use her occult powers to achieve the desired results. It was said that Lena was descended from numerous practitioners of the black arts and so had grown up learning the secrets of the craft and how to use them to work on others. Or at least that's what many residents of the area must have thought when they heard about Florence's difficulties, and what Mode Auman said about them.

Another witch on her broomstick. Popular depiction of a witch riding her broomstick through tempestuous skies. (Based on an 1800 engraving – photo of a public domain postcard from Zazzle.)

"One night, Florence went out to the barn to do the feedin' and the damn cow pinned her against the wall," recalled our storyteller as he began his unusual narrative, which was typical of many witch tales that were once popular and often widely believed throughout the Pennsylvania mountains.

"The fella she was goin' with happened to be with her, and he went in and got her away and took her up to old Mode. They said old Mode Auman was one of those brauchers too. Old Mode looked at her and said, 'Well, there's things goin' on here that you can't do much with. I'll see what I can do. Now there's nothin' I can do now; this is done, but I'll keep track.'

"So, one night she went out to do the feedin', and the damn cow got after her again! So they went back up to Auman, and he was supposed to take a deck of cards and pull a card out of it."[2]

At this point our storyteller's wife took up the narrative, because she had heard the rest of the story from her grandfather, Ira Lingle, who claimed to have seen the effects of Mode Auman's use of playing cards to cast a counterspell on Ira's mother Lena.

---

2. Ibid.

"Well, her ears got burnt off," explained Ira Lingle's granddaughter, as she proceeded to tell us the rest of the story. "I don't know, but somethin' happened and she just caught on fire! Grandpa said she was standin' there in front of one of them old cook stoves and she just caught on fire. And he said she did like this [covered her ears with her hands], and her ears burnt off her head! I remember seein' the cook stove. I was little, but I remember seein' it.

"But grandpa said that after that she never went out without a bandanna wrapped around her head; she was never seen without a scarf or hat pulled down over her ears! Everyone noticed that she must not have any ears and thought that proved she was a witch! And when she was buried he said they had to have a rag to wrap around her head so you couldn't see her ears!"[3]

THAWING THINGS OUT OR KNOCKING THEM ABOUT

One of my favorite witch stories is an anecdote I collected down in York County in 1997 when I was living in Lancaster County. That county, and its neighbors, still contained a treasure trove of all kinds of supernatural-type tales at that time, mainly because those who first settled the area in the 1700s were immigrants from Germany who brought these kinds of stories with them from the Old Country.

Superstitions and belief in witchcraft lingered longer in the Pennsylvania Dutch counties than anywhere else in the state, and the following tale is typical of many of the same type that once could be heard here. However, it too shows how superstition quite often managed to push common sense and consideration of logical explanations aside when it came to explaining events that at first glance appeared to be supernatural. In this case, the story my narrator told to me was a tale he had heard "a lot of times" from his father. Theodore Landis, born in 1920, had in turn heard it firsthand from his father-in-law, Rubin Kampbell.

Rubin Kampbell lived on a little farm close to the small town of Locust Grove, which today could almost be considered a suburb of the city of York, in York County. Of course, at this period, during the late 1800s, this same area was mostly picturesque farmland, characterized by small family

3. Mrs. Ray Rowles, recorded July 27, 1983, July 5, 1984, and May 26, 1988.

farms and expansive fields tilled and planted by machinery pulled by teams of horses.

Living in the middle of this scenic terrain was an old woman whose small house sat on a hill next to one of the Kampbells' fields. She seemed harmless enough at first, but then one day the Kampbells couldn't get their cream to turn to butter, and soon thereafter Rubin's team of horses suddenly got a stubborn streak.

"They could churn and churn and churn, and it would never get butter," claimed the old man whose grandfather had to decide how to remedy the problem with his wife's churn.

Soon afterwards the York County farmer noticed that whenever he would plow the field right below the old crone's house on the hill, his team of horses would stop in its tracks whenever it got to a certain spot in the field.

"Then they heard that old Mrs. Fry, their neighbor up on the hill, could witch people," recalled our storyteller. "But the way I used to hear it, if you knew what to do, you could break any spell that someone put on ya," he went on as he entertained us with this tale of a unique time in Pennsylvania's storied past.

"Anyway, he found out that the next time the team stopped there, he should just unhook 'em, then take 'em into the barn. Then he was to bring straw out and put it around the plow and light it. And they said whoever's doing it will come to your place. So he did this.

"And two or three days later this lady on the hill come down there to their place, and she had both her arms wrapped up. And they asked her what happened, and she said 'Ah, I burnt myself.'

"After that he could plow. It never happened again. I guess she got sorta wise that they mighta known she was doin' it. Anyway, it didn't happen after that. But they still couldn't make butter afterwards. I mean they didn't find out what to do to break that spell, but they could never make butter. I mean they could churn it and churn it, and it never made butter. But he got that fixed so that he could plow!"[4]

Not too long after telling us about how his grandfather's horses were hexed by the spell of the old witch who lived on a hill near Locust Grove in York County, our storyteller proceeded to tell us another tale about a

---

4. Ted Landis (born 1920), recorded October 19, 1997.

team of horses that also occasionally refused to move. In this case, however, the man driving the team knew better than to assume the horses had been rendered immobile, or become fastened in the terminology of witchcraft, by the evil spell of a witch. He was, in fact, aware of an entirely different, more natural, explanation.

"I know my dad said he was mowin' a hay field one time with a team, and he saw a black snake, and the team stopped. When they would see a snake, the team would stop dead. He knew the team wouldn't move when there was a snake around somewhere! He couldn't move the team until the snake went away."[5]

This last story made us wonder why Rubin Kampbell hadn't considered the same explanation when his team of horses stopped dead every time they came to the same spot in one of his fields. However, his failure to consider this alternative explanation wasn't entirely Mr. Kampbell's fault. The combination of deep-seated superstitions and limited education was a powerful force that often overwhelmed rational judgment in those days, and this was a condition not just confined to York County.

Around the same time that Rubin Kampbell was dealing with his diabolical neighbor, a Clinton County man was having similar problems. Living along the West Branch of the Susquehanna River in those days was a lad whose daily work routine would always take him through the small village of Charlton. He initially had no problems in making that trip, but, according to local tales, the carefree young man eventually began to dread the drive through the little hamlet. It seems that his horse suddenly decided that it needed to stop at the same spot about halfway through town every day. Here it would stand and refuse to budge, no matter how much coaxing or whipping would be showered upon it.

Finally, the frustrated horseman decided to confide in his elderly aunt, who, he knew, was well versed in such matters. After telling her the details of his daily aggravation, the old woman solemnly declared that she'd "put a fix to that."

"The next time that horse stops in front of the house," she instructed, "you get out and knock two spokes out of the back wagon wheel."

This the young man did, and two days later when he drove through town, he saw an old woman come out of a house that was next to the place

---

5. Ibid.

in the road where his horse would always stop. Much to his surprise, he recognized her as the mother of a young lady in whom he had no interest, but who, he knew, had a crush on him. Even more surprising was the fact, evidenced by the splints and slings she was wearing, that she had evidently somehow broken both of her arms.

It didn't take long for the harried driver of the horse and wagon to realize that the injured lady was a witch who had put a hex on his horse so that it would always stop in front of her house. She had hoped, he later concluded, that during this interlude he would get to know her daughter better and take a liking to her. The old hex's spell to fasten his horses had worked for a while, but when a stronger counterspell was cast against her, so people thought, two broken arms was the price she paid for her meddling.[6]

PIGHEADED OR JUST BEWITCHED?

Butchering time, people used to believe, was a period when practitioners of the black arts were at their most active. The evildoers seemed to enjoy practicing their devilish ways then because of the frustration they could create. After all, when a farmer was trying to butcher an animal to feed his family, he would find it quite annoying when he couldn't do so because he couldn't kill the animal in the first place. And at one time the Pennsylvania hills were rife with such stories, particularly tales of how butchering of a bewitched hog was delayed until, thanks to a counterspell, a bullet finally took effect and put the animal down.

One such tale comes out of Krise Valley, in Centre County. This relatively unsettled region is one of my favorite spots in the Pennsylvania mountains because of its many dark hollows and its mist-filled ravines. It is a place any lover of wild regions should soon go to explore and to enjoy, especially since the Pennsylvania Department of Transportation is considering, in their callous way, ripping through it when current Route 322 is widened and rerouted. One can only imagine what it must have been like here a hundred years ago around butchering time when smoke from the fires under black cast-iron kettles drifted into the dense forest of the valley.

"I've heard of 'em butcherin' already and they come to kill a hog," said the lifelong Krise Valley native, who "heard the older fellas tellin' this story."

---

6. Bill Simcox (born 1934), recorded January 9, 2000.

Witches at their cauldron. Illustration from an 1864 Strand Theatre program for Shakespeare's Macbeth. *Scene is based on Act iv, Scene 1 and is titled "Twice the Brindled Cat Hath Mew'd." Illustrator unknown.*

"They'd shoot and shoot, and the hog would just squeal. Well, the lady come out there and she had her apron all rolled up in her hand. She said, 'You can't kill that hog!'

"And he kept shootin', and every time the hog would squeal. So after a bit she just left go or her apron and it unrolled. Then she said, 'Now you can kill it!', and the first shot they shot they killed the hog!"[7]

Down along the "crick road" of eastern Penn's Valley, Centre County, there was once another pig that refused to die at butchering time. The following tale is just another typical variation of the last story. In this case our narrator saw the events firsthand.

"I saw a guy one time shoot a pig seven times in the same place before it went down," recalled the old farmer.

"And the last time he shot it, he stuck the bullet in his mouth before he put it in the gun. And when they butchered the hog, they cut the head up and found all seven bullets had hit the same place in that hog's head

7. Vince Treaster (born 1922), recorded November 5, 1988.

before it went down! The funny part was that hog never squealed and never moved. It just stood there. Every time the gun would crack he'd just shake his head.

"Then the guy said, 'Well I'm a son of a bitch, you will go down!', and he took the shell and put it in his mouth and swirled it around and put 'er in, and when the gun cracked, down he went. That makes the hair stand up on the back of your head!"[8]

Still one more tale from the same area provides yet another flavor of this old-time favorite. The source of this story was said to be old-time braucher Bennie Ripka of Spring Mills, Centre County, a man I've mentioned in many of my other witch tales.

"I did hear of Bennie sayin' that he was at a butcherin' once and they couldn't shoot the pigs," noted our seventy-three-year-old informant.

"He said the bullets just dropped out the end of the gun barrel and down into the hog pen! He said he took the butcher knife that they wanted to use to stick the pig and stuck it in the top of a post along the outside of the hog pen. Then he just walked away."

Those at the butchering must have been duly impressed when the next shot killed the hog. It was enough to impress our storyteller, who believed that Bennie's actions "must've broke somethin'," and that "all Bennie needed to do was to be there; that made the difference!"[9]

At first glance it would appear that supernatural influences sometimes take control when someone tries to shoot a pig at butchering time, but those who are familiar about such matters know that it's not always that easy to down a hog with a bullet. Just like the old gentleman who had attended many butcherings in his day; and who, to his dying day, remembered one pig that had to be shot "thirteen or sixteen times" before they killed it.[10]

Those who are aware of some of the anatomical features of the pig claim to know the logical explanation for why bullets sometimes don't penetrate its skull. According to one such individual who explained the finer points to me, apparently the animals sometimes can actually have "double skulls" that make their heads "bulletproof," and in the cases where the skulls are normal there are only a few vulnerable spots that are not strong enough to resist penetration by a bullet.

8. Ray Rowles (born 1933), recorded July 27, 1983, July 5, 1984, and May 26, 1988.
9. Wilbur Auman (born 1915), recorded November 19, 1988.
10. Paul Zerby (born 1919), recorded August 6, 2000.

So, the pig's seeming resistance to bullets is not a matter of witch-craft after all. Nonetheless, the old-timers, who believed that witches were behind it all, would probably still not have been easily convinced that sci-ence had a better explanation. Instead, they would have been more likely to resort to their own means to solve the problem; perhaps even trying to use the renowned remedy of "driving in the peg"—a procedure that's recalled in the next story.

DRIVING IN THE PEG

"An old witch can kill ya'!" claimed the eighty-two-year-old resident of a remote valley lying in the heart of the Centre County mountains. And this was said in 1988, by a man who was entirely convinced that witches were real, and that their abilities to cast awful hexes on others were just as real. "Do you know how they do it?" he asked us in all sincerity.

"Why, they stop your bowel movement," he went on without missing a beat. This led him to a story about a man he knew, who was friends with a man who had been hexed in such a way by his neighbor after hard feel-ings arose between them. According to our storyteller's recollection, the two men joined forces and "worked on" the neighbor until they "stopped his bowel movement." "Yeah, that's true," concluded the old man. "They stopped his bowel movement and he got yellow in the face; and they killed him!"[11]

Witches, it was believed, could supposedly be killed by supernatu-ral means too. One such technique was that of "driving in the peg," as described in the following tale. It is a story which I also collected in Centre County, but it is followed by a similar tale I collected down in Cumberland County, and then by another Centre County tale that says that witches would sometimes take steps to prevent the driving of the peg.

Apparently, sometime in the distant past, a resident of one of the iso-lated valleys in the Seven Mountains section of Centre County thought he had been hexed by a local witch. Deciding that a local braucher would be able to help him out, he went to him and explained his problems.

"He wrote something on a piece of paper," said our storyteller of many old-time witch tales, who was explaining to us what instructions the braucher passed on to his client. "And then he told him that he then had

---

11. Randall Steiger (born 1904), recorded November 15, 1980, June 4, 1982, and May 4, 1988.

a drill a hole in a tree and get a dowel that fit that hole," continued our entertaining host.

"When you had that done you had to put the paper in the hole and use the dowel to hammer it in all the way. Once't you got that hammered in tight, why, he said that would kill the witch!"

The braucher's client decided to carry out the instructions he was given, and so drilled a hole in a tree and got a wooden dowel rod that was the same size as the hole. Then he shoved the paper the braucher had given him into the hole in the tree, stuck the dowel into the hole, and began to hammer it in all the way.

"While this guy was hammerin' this pin in," noted our storyteller as he concluded his tale, "he said his wallet flew out of his pocket, and the papers in it flew all around. But he kept right on goin' 'til he was done. He said the next morning the fella that was doin' the hexin' didn't get up!"[12]

A slightly different approach to the peg technique was once used down in Cumberland County, where it is said a large iron nail or spike rather than a wooden peg could be used to achieve less deadly, but similar results.

"My great-grandmother was a witch doctor or powwower, or whatever you wanta call them," said the Cumberland County farmer. "She had neighbors, Carbaugh was their name I believe, who had these cattle that were sick and dying. He came to her, and, of course, she told him how to go about getting rid of the evil spell that he believed had been cast upon his cows.

"He was to get a spike and take it down in the meadow where he pastured his cattle and drive the spike part way into a tree. Every time he took his cattle down or brought them back, he was to drive that spike further into the tree.

"She said 'Just take one swing at it, and if you miss it, why you mustn't swing at it a second time. And when that spike is driven into the tree, the person who put the spell on your cattle will come and offer to pay for them.'

"But he wasn't to take the payment, because if he did that would nullify the spell" noted the grandson of the woman who passed on these instructions to her neighbor with the sick cows.

"Yeah, and they came," concluded the braucher's descendant. "They found out it was his brother!"[13]

12. Ray Rowles, Ibid.
13. Ray Waggoner (born 1926), recorded February 17, 1980.

Of course, popular superstition also held that witches would not always sit by and let someone try to kill them, and one Centre County episode illustrates that belief. It seems that a woman who lived near the small village of Coburn in the early years of the twentieth century became deathly ill one day, and as time went by none of her doctor's medicines seemed to bring relief. Finally, one of her relatives convinced the rest of the family that she had been bewitched by a neighbor woman, whose family and that of the sick woman's had harbored bad feelings about one another for years.

This same relative went on to explain that he had once heard of a procedure that might counteract the neighbor woman's spell. He said the first thing to do would be to drill three holes in the north side of a pine tree and then get three wooden pegs that would fit into the holes. Then on a moonless night the three wooden pegs should be driven into the holes, saying "Father" when the first was driven in, "Son" when the second was driven, and "Holy Ghost" for the third.

It was agreed that the man should make the necessary preparations and drive the pegs on the next moonless night. On that night when no moon could be seen in the sky, the man took his pegs to the tree where he had drilled three holes. He drove in the first peg, and then the second, reciting the appropriate holy words according to the directions as he remembered them. However, just as he was inserting the third plug into its hole, a black cat darted out of the darkest part of the nearby forest and ran into his leg. The cat then took off down a nearby alley, and the driver of the pegs noticed that it ran into the yard of the suspected hex woman.

This unexpected distraction broke the rhythm of the proceedings, and so he knew that he'd have to be satisfied with the results two pegs would produce. Two were apparently effective enough, because the next morning the sick woman's family found out that their unfriendly neighbor lady had taken ill. Now she was also under a doctor's care; and it was, they believed, all because of driving some pegs into a tree.[14]

_____

14. Dorothy C. Meyer, *Legends and Lore of Centre County*, Chapter 14.

CHAPTER 6

THE OLD IRON BELL

Sometimes the currents of change, which we like to call progress, wash away chronicles of past events and places so thoroughly that the historical record is swept clean, robbing future generations of one more link to their increasingly distant heritage. Certainly, there are many cases that could be cited as examples. Links in many tenuous historical chains have been broken due to the way progress runs roughshod over anything that gets in its way.

Occasionally, however, in a headlong rush through the portals of time that lead to the uncertain future, the torrents of change will sometimes indiscriminately dislodge some of the weakest historical links rather than drowning them out. This is why the links to seemingly insignificant events and place names sometimes manage to float through portals to the future as well. And that is why it is a pleasant surprise when someone can find such links, reconnect them, and follow the reconstructed chain back to another place and time.

One such chain was discovered almost a half century ago, and it led to a revival in interest about the history, stories, and legends surrounding a dilapidated log building that stood almost forgotten along the base of Brush Mountain in Centre County for nearly two hundred years. Known to locals as the remains of one of the old settlers' forts in Penn's Valley, Centre County, scholars were not so sure. The highbrows even debated whether or not there ever was such a citadel as the so-called "middle" fort, but then historian Charles F. Snyder settled the dispute once and for all.

Through hours of painstaking research and study of local maps, the tireless antiquarian finally proved that the deteriorating pile of logs was indeed exactly what locals had known all along.

The antiquarian's findings resulted in an eleventh-hour reprieve for the old landmark, because had it not been for Snyder's efforts the old bastion would have gradually decayed to the point where all traces of it had disappeared altogether. Once that had happened there is little doubt that historians would have felt justified in considering tales of its existence to be little more than a figment from the imagination of either a romantic novelist or an inventive chronicler of the olden days.

Historical records indicate beyond doubt that there were, during the times of the Indian wars, two other forts in the valley besides the middle one. However, these other two were more secure in their provenance. Their locations were well known, and some historical accounts of them were well documented in history books.

The upper, or Potter's Fort, for example, was historically grounded because General James Potter of Revolutionary War fame was instrumental in building the place. Likewise, the memory of the lower, or Stover's Fort, although not quite as assured of its place in history as that of General Potter's, was kept alive by the valley's folktales about Jacob Stover, "the man who couldn't be shot" (see the author's story entitled "The Lower Fort" in *Volume II*).

The middle fort, on the other hand, had no such extraordinary individuals to insure that a memory of the place would be preserved in historical records or folktales of the area. Therefore, if it had not been mentioned in letters written by soldiers who had been stationed at the place they called "Fort Watson" there would have been no clues a dogged historian like Charles Snyder could have used to track down the elusive historical site. If that had been the case, then historians would have certainly discredited locals' claims that the site was hallowed ancestral ground. They would have stated that such a place never existed, except in someone's imagination, and then even the legend about the fort would have fared no better, gradually being discredited as well.

There are no local tales of great battles that ever took place at Fort Watson, and consequently no accounts of great heroes who were associated with the bastion. Mention of the fort is conspicuously missing from local historical records and from accounts of Pennsylvania's Indian wars, and even *Frontier Forts of Pennsylvania*, the official compendium of the state's frontier strongholds, has nothing to say about the place.

It's not surprising, then, that knowledge of the fort's location languished for decades until Charles Snyder found the ruins. What is surprising, however, is how the fort's discovery also brought about another discovery which led to a rebirth of the fort's legend.

Not long after the fort was discovered, sitting close by a mountain farmhouse in Penn's Valley, a related event occurred in an antique shop in the small village of Coburn, Centre County. It appears that for years an old iron bell sat on a back shelf of the shop, where it had been ignored by buyers for so long that it was destined to land in the hands of a scrap metal dealer. Dusty and forgotten, the heavy relic had been passed over by

The Indian alarm. Not the old iron bell used at Fort Watson, but one very similar.

countless antique hunters, until one day a party of local historical buffs spotted it and asked about its history.

It was, they were told by the shop owner, "once used as the alarm bell in old Fort Watson." The information struck a chord with the antiquarians, and they purchased the bell on the spot. They also made the county newspaper aware of their good luck, and the editor sent out a reporter to obtain further details for an article. During the course of his research, the local reporter interviewed a number of the valley's older residents, and it was then that the legend of the bell came to light.

The old legend had almost been forgotten by this time, but a few old-timers, once their memories were jogged, could recall their parents talking about the bell, and how it was at one time mounted on the roof of the fort where it served a dual purpose. It seems that in times of peace it was used to call field workers in for meals or for sounding fire alarms, but during the times of the Indian wars the bell was rung to warn settlers that parties of marauding Indians had been seen in the area.

When the bell sounded an Indian alarm, the valley's nearby settlers would rush to the safety of the fortress, where they would often successfully "weather out" the impending dreadnought until the Indians gave up and left in disgust. It was a defensive maneuver that apparently worked quite well for the area's brave pioneers for some time because no records of any massacres were ever recorded in this part of the valley. However, it must have been a very frustrating and humiliating situation for the Indians because, according to the legend, they eventually decided they needed to do something about the bell.

The legend doesn't say how long it took the Indians to come up with their plan, but apparently one dark night during one of the last years of the Revolutionary War, a small band of Indians could be seen creeping stealthily up to the sides of the log structure. Since they had not been spotted when they came into the area, an alarm had never been sounded, and so Fort Watson, so named because it was on the farm of early settler John Watson, was deserted that night. In fact, the distant barking of a dog would probably have been the only sound to disturb the stillness of the mountains as one of the Indians scaled the log walls of the fort and climbed onto its roof.

It was not until several days later, when perhaps Mrs. Watson herself tried to ring the bell to call the farm hands in for the noon meal, that it was discovered the bell wouldn't make a sound. Further investigation revealed that the clapper was missing, and despite a concerted search of the grounds around the fort, it could not be found.

The settlers were no doubt at first puzzled by the strange disappearance, but eventually they all must have agreed that only the Indians would have the motive for stealing the clapper, and only the Indians were well versed enough and well-practiced enough in stealthy raiding tactics to do so. Although their final conclusions were probably hotly debated for many successive generations, the historical records of Pennsylvania's early pioneer days and of the accompanying Indian wars tend to support the old settlers' views.[1] Moreover there are at least two Centre County traditions that show how stealthy and how bold some Indians could be in those days, even in times of peace.

For generations there has been a tradition passed down through members of the Wilson family of Halfmoon Township, Centre County, about how their Quaker ancestors were awakened on several occasions by several stalwart Indian braves who managed to infiltrate their premises without a sound. George Wilson and his wife believed, as staunch advocates of William Penn's faith, that they should always help others whenever possible.

Their stalwart faith led them to believe that their doors should always be left unlocked in case a wayfaring stranger might need a place for the night, and so the Wilsons only latched their doors before retiring, despite the fact that some of those wayfaring strangers might be Indians, who could still be seen passing through here in the last decade of the 1700s.

The Wilsons were the first settlers in the little valley, and so had no one else to depend upon for defense except themselves. But at that late date the Indians were on peaceful terms with the settlers, and so the Wilsons had little fear of attacks. However, the family eventually began to get an uneasy feeling that all was not as secure as they might like it to be.

If it had only been a single occurrence, the Wilsons may have just ignored it, but on several different times they were awakened by a strong musky smell coming from downstairs. The first several times they noticed

---

1. "Symbol of Rivalry Once Told of Danger," *Centre Daily Times*, State College, PA, 1974. Here it is also noted that the bell was, at that time, used as a trophy in an annual football contest between the Penns Valley and Bald Eagle Area High Schools.

the strange odor they were too tired to look into it and just ignored it, but one cold rainy night when the smell was particularly strong, George Wilson went down to investigate.

Much to the old Quaker's dismay, he found two husky Indian braves huddled by the massive stone fireplace in the kitchen. They were fast asleep and had evidently decided they would come inside to a warmer and drier bed, just like they must have done on previous nights when the Wilsons noticed their body odor. With that revelation, the Wilsons decided to finally put a sturdy bolted lock on the door of their beautiful stone house, and once it was installed they made sure it was securely fastened in place every single night thereafter.[2]

There is another Centre County stone house dating back to Colonial days whose residents once had problems with local Indians too. Probably built sometime in the 1790s, this large limestone block building was originally the home of state senator Andrew Gregg and his family. The old water pump out back, and the adjacent weathered outbuildings, add to the feeling that one is stepping back into the past as you travel up the remote country road leading to the farmhouse. Virtually unchanged since it was built, the house has five fireplaces besides the huge walk-in fireplace in the main kitchen. Another feature of the old manse is its summer kitchen, where the Greggs would often hang their grain to dry.

Similar to the Wilsons, the Greggs, too, would sometimes have nocturnal visits from local Indians who knew about the drying grain in the summer kitchen. The friendly natives would on dark nights, claimed the Greggs in tales they passed on to their descendants, emerge from the woods back of the Gregg's home and sneak into the summer kitchen. They would then help themselves to shocks of dried yellow grain hanging from the massive dark brown ceiling beams that had been fashioned from giant oak trees that grew on the property.[3]

Centre County is not alone in its popular stories about Indians who helped themselves to white men's things without asking. According to a narrative from neighboring Clinton County, interactions between Indians and occupants of a settlers' fort could sometimes take an unusual twist, particularly when the Indians saw something that caught their fancy, and

---

2. Dorothy C. Meyer, "Descendant Lives on Pioneer's Site," *Centre Daily Times*, State College, PA, 1975.

3. Charles C. Dubois, "Team Measuring History" *Centre Daily Times*, State College, PA, 1975; Reverend John Heckewelder, *History, Manner, and Customs of the Indian Nations*, 329.

they decided to just help themselves. (Although they're not intended that way, the preceding sentences sound like an attempt to defame and tarnish the reputations of Pennsylvania's Native Americans. Therefore, in order to rectify that thought, it's probably good to remind the reader that sharing all they had, even with strangers, was part of the Native American culture. It's therefore not surprising that they would assume that their European neighbors were just as gracious.)

One of the most exciting events recorded in the annals of the West Branch Valley's pioneer days was the incident known as the Big Runaway. The entire frontier region here was alarmed, during June of 1778, by rumors of an Indian uprising to the northeast. Descriptions of the panic and mass exodus that subsequently occurred along the Susquehanna's West Branch have come down to the present day from the lips of none other than frontier ranger Robert Covenhoven. His account has led historians to suggest that the Big Runaway was not only a time of terror, but also an event that, others may agree, "has no parallel in frontier history."[4]

At that time of upheaval, a substantial pioneer fortress known as Reed's Fort stood on ground where the present-day town of Lock Haven now sits. The fort was guarded by a "fearless few" and commanded by Colonel Cookson Long. Named for William Reed, owner of the land on which the fortress was built, the bastion never had more than fifteen men that could be included in its garrison. And of those troops, it is said that William Reed and his five sons constituted one-third of the fighting force, with the Flemings making up most of the remaining count.

During the Big Runaway, Reed's Fort was abandoned, along with settlers' houses, barns, and other outbuildings, for a period of five years before the frontiersmen felt safe enough to return to their former homes. Most of the homes had not been destroyed by the Indians, and standing as a testament to the quality construction principles of the settlers, many of them had withstood the ravages of the weather quite well too. All the settlers went to work with a will to put their log cabins back in order, but, since it was the most substantially built, the house of William Reed was completed first.

Times of comparative peace settled upon the region after this, and the settlers here were often visited by friendly Indians, who they always

---

4. Thomas L. Montgomery, ed., *Frontier Forts of Pennsylvania, Volume I*, 412–13.

Remains of old Fort Watson, Centre County. This is the site where the old fort once stood and where its remains could be found for many years. The spring used as its water source still flows there today.

treated kindly, generously providing them with food and other handouts when they came around. The Reed family was no exception, and William's daughter Jane, who seems to have been chief cook for both her father's family and the garrison of soldiers that might be in the fort at any one time, repeatedly exhausted her entire supply of bread in feeding straggling bands of Indians.

Miss Reed not only was frequently provoked by the seemingly ungrateful attitude of the Indians toward her largess, but would also become overly stressed when she had a scanty supply of bread on hand, and the Indians would suddenly make an appearance. She knew it gave them offence if they were not all treated alike; and when supplies were short, she was often at wits' end to know how to dole out her bread so all would get an equal share.

Then the proverbial straw that broke the camel's back fell upon Jane one day, when some Indians unexpectedly entered the Reed cabin while she was trying on a new hat she had just purchased. After gazing with astonishment at the head cover, one of the bolder warriors walked over, took the hat from Miss Reed's head, inspected it, and then passed it over to his companions for them to inspect. After each in turn had scrutinized it, they placed the hat back on Jane's head and departed, showing no interest in appropriating the new-fangled headdress.

Miss Jane's opinion of the Indians had never been a very exalted one, but now it had reached its nadir, and so when one morning she found a mouse drowned in her cream pot she decided to churn some of the impure liquid into butter and save the rest. The next time the Indians paid her a visit it is said that she "had the grim satisfaction of seeing them feast on butter and buttermilk to their heart's content."[5]

One of the earliest settlers along the Conococheague Creek in Franklin County took sterner measures to prevent his Indian neighbors from feeling that they could just help themselves to any of his produce or belongings any time they wanted. Benjamin Chambers always managed to maintain a friendly intercourse with the Indians in his vicinity. He developed a lively trade with them and had earned their trust. However, he wasn't quite yet sure how far he could trust them, particularly after he saw some of them secretly stalking through the thickets surrounding the meadow where he was making hay one afternoon.

Chambers actually became alarmed when he noticed the Indians were still concealed in the thickets as darkness began to fall. Unleashing two of his most ferocious dogs, Chambers and the canines gave chase to the Indians. The warriors escaped, but later acknowledged that they had gone to the meadow to steal Chambers' ornate gold watch, which they admired, and to carry off his Negro servant woman, who they thought would be useful in helping them raise their corn.[6]

Based on the true accounts passed down to the present day by the descendants of the Wilsons, Greggs, Reeds, and Chambers, there is support for the belief that Indians not only walked away with the spoils of war when they raided settlements, but sometimes filched settlers' belongings in times of peace as well.

Accepting that practice as a possibility, then it's perhaps also possible that the iron bell on top of old Fort Watson in Centre County was coveted in different ways by both friendly and hostile Indians. In the first case, the peaceful types may have just been fascinated enough with the bell to want a piece of it for themselves (although it would have been a useless

5. William H. Egle, *History of the Commonwealth of Pennsylvania*, 576.
6. Ibid, 744.

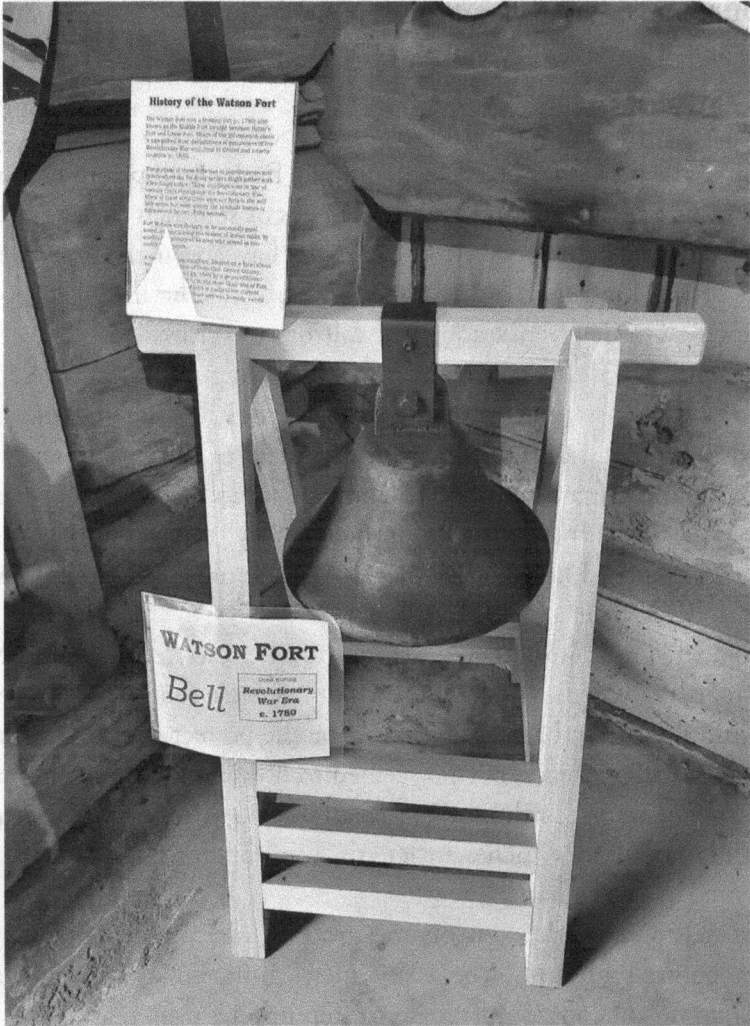

The old iron bell. This bell sits in the museum of the Penns Valley Area Historical Museum Association, Aaronsburg, Centre County. For years it sat in a trophy case at Bald Eagle Area High School as a victory prize awarded to the winner of the Old Iron Bell annual football contest between Penns Valley and Bald Eagle Area High Schools. Once its true origins became known, the two high schools agreed it should be turned over to the Museum in Aaronsburg and a replica provided to Bald Eagle High School. Interestingly enough, this ancient relic's clapper is missing!

and impractical souvenir for the sons of the forest). Bellicose types, on the other hand, may have considered the bell a nuisance and merely wanted to nullify its power as an alarm.

Whatever the case may have been, the bell, if it was mounted on the rooftop of the fort, might have been unique. Early descriptions of Pennsylvania's frontier forts mention nightly watches or sentinels that were posted to detect Indian raiders, but this seems to have been the only warning system of any kind that is mentioned, other than the use of dogs and a cruel method of deterrence known as caltrops or "crowsfeet."

Around 1763 the commander of Fort Augusta, near present-day Sunbury, was frustrated by the boldness of hostile Indians who always seemed to be harassing the fort from the safety of the bushes and woods surrounding it. After a number of incidents where Fort Augusta sentinels were picked off by Indian snipers and retaliatory troops sent out from the fort were ambushed, the commander decided to use a crueler and deadlier means of deterrence.

Colonel James Burd ordered that caltrops be scattered along those areas most frequented by the Indians, knowing that these four-pronged pieces of iron with their sharp barbed tips would be the perfect countermeasure for fending off Indian attackers who seemed to hold no fear of his troops and their armaments. Accordingly, the deadly devices, with each iron prong measuring about four inches in length, were scattered around the areas frequented by the Indians.

No matter how they sat on the ground, one of the caltrop's sharp prongs pointed upward. The rusty metal inflicted a horribly painful wound upon someone unfortunate to step upon a prong, and, except for cutting it out, it was impossible to remove. The caltrop left its victims crippled for some time if they survived at all. Often its victims succumbed to tetanus-induced lockjaw or other infections that came from cutting out the rusty barbed object. In later years souvenir hunters would find these devices in the fields surrounding Fort Augusta, unpleasant reminders of man's inhumanity to man.

No caltrops, or similar relics, were ever found around Fort Watson. But it's doubtful if a fort that small would have used caltrops, since farmers here probably pastured their livestock nearby. On the other hand, perhaps the old iron alarm bell that was supposedly mounted on the roof of the fort was deterrent enough to keep the Indians at bay. Even if that were true, however, the bell couldn't provide protection from one other determined force—the unrelenting destructive powers of Mother Nature.

When I visited the remains of the old fort one April day about thirty years ago, I was disappointed to find that there were no longer any of its wooden timbers or beams left. The farmer who owned the land there recalled to us that after the roof fell in, the logs "had started to go" quickly. Regardless of that, the practical farmer, true to his Pennsylvania Dutch heritage, explained that he had decided to use them before they could rot away entirely. Consequently, most of them were used over the years as "butcher wood" to heat the large black iron kettles used for cooking meat and rendering lard at butchering time. But that supply had lasted a long time.

"And then here last spring, we had it dozed up," declared our host. "It got kinda dangerous, and it kept growing up in weeds," he continued. "You couldn't do anything with it anymore. So we got four truckloads! But it was made completely out of logs with a second story; and was probably twenty by thirty. On the inside there was no partition in it, but there were steps inside the first story that went upstairs. It was a complete one floor on the top and one floor on the bottom."[7]

It was a disappointment to us to find out we'd missed seeing the last remaining logs of the old fortress by just a year. However, a high stone wall that led from where the bastion once stood to a nearby spring was still standing. Our friendly informant explained that he recalled when there had been another wall that ran parallel to the one that was still there. The two walls were about three feet apart, and, our host was certain, they had both been about six feet high.

"I can remember because I could walk through there and the rocks were higher than my head,"[8] he explained.

He went on to explain that they had been built as a further means of protecting the settlers who had forted there during an Indian invasion. Whenever the fort's defenders ran out of water, they were assured of a safe route to the cool waters of the spring because of the protected passageway afforded by the stone walls.

---

7. William Crater (born 1935), recorded April 22, 1990.
8. Ibid.

The Indians had their own defenses. Model of palisadid Indian stockade enclosing Indian long houses. Native Americans in Pennsylvania did not live in wigwams, but instead built long rectangular houses made from wood. This representation of one such Indian village shows how they protected themselves from wild animals. It sits inside the museum at the Conrad Weiser Homestead historical site at Womelsdorf in Berks County.

The fact that there was still some evidence left of one of Pennsylvania's original settlers' forts was extremely satisfying to those of us who loved to track down such things. However, it was disheartening to know that the fort itself had been bulldozed down and carted away as rubbish. Not a very honorable ending for a structure that had no doubt protected many families from scalping parties who had nothing to offer except a tomahawk's crushing blows or a scalping knife's swift cuts. At the very least the middle fort should have been commemorated in verse, just as a memory of the upper fort was preserved by Centre Hall's Harvey Wagner Flink in the following poem, which Flink titled "Old Fort Hill."

Tonight the moon is redder
Than a bowl of human blood,
And, low and full, it lightens
The dusk-hung neighborhood.

The sultry air is throbbing
   To an unheard tom-tom beat;
The tall dead grass is swishing
   Beneath the tread of feet.
And here I linger, watching
   Dim, warlike forms advance,
For on Old Fort Hilltop
   The ghosts of Indians dance.[9]

NOTE: Those who would like to see the old iron bell that came from the antique shop in Coburn should pay a visit to the museum in Aaronsburg. There is no date on the bell, but its inscription does say it was made in Reading by the Eagle Iron Works. There is also no clapper in the bell, which is to be expected if it is the same bell featured in the legend about it. Those who have time and who want to verify the specifics of that legend may want to see if the iron works noted on the bell could have made it around the same time that it was supposedly fitted on Fort Watson's rooftop. If the date fits, then that would appear to be the final link in an historical chain that connects the present day to the thrilling times of old Fort Watson when Indians and settlers battled for the right to call the region's beautiful valleys and mountains their own.

9. W. W. Kerlin, ed., *Centre Hall, Centre County, Pennsylvania*, 333.

CHAPTER 7

GIVE ME THE
GOOD OLD DAYS

Good fortune for any collectors of quaint and forgotten lore comes with a price. A large collection means that the hunting has been good, and many old-time stories will be preserved for posterity. However, in any large assortment of anecdotes there are inevitably some that, if taken individually, are too short to fill an entire chapter on their own. Many of these are just too valuable to discard. Each is worth preserving because it holds a unique and pleasant picture of days gone by; saves a little piece of the Good Old Days that otherwise might be lost forever. And in this chapter are some of those types of mementoes; little gems that I just couldn't bear to see discarded and forgotten.

Just like the other accounts in the *Pennsylvania Fireside Tales* series, these anecdotes evoke images in our minds of a Pennsylvania of ninety or more years ago. However, the common trait that characterizes these tales is humor. Taken as a whole, they show us that despite the hard times of the Good Old Days, people still could find something to laugh at. Even death, that feared Harvester of town and country folk alike, was not exempt from being the subject of a funny story. And if Pennsylvanians of seventy-five or more years ago could laugh at death, it shows that they must have indeed had a sense of humor we can still appreciate today.

A NIGHT TO REMEMBER
(Setting: the 1930s, near the village of Seven Stars, Blair County)
"Poode" Eyer knew first-hand that Sarley Leach wasn't the cleanest fella you'd ever meet. Sarley was an old hermit who stayed in a shack in the foothills of Tussey Mountain near the small town of Pine Grove Mills in Centre County, and his ramshackle house gave passersby a hint as to the care its lone inhabitant neglected to give to himself.

Remembered as being unkempt and dirty, Sarley's other outstanding characteristics were his body odor (or to put it in the words of a popular saying of the times, "he smelled so bad he could chase a maggot off a gut wagon"), and his penchant for strong liquor. He was also a regular visitor to the town of Tyrone in Blair County, where he would go to shop for groceries; and without fail his shopping list always included a stop at the local hotel for a few drinks. Perhaps it was the regular exercise he got from his walks into Tyrone that kept the old man physically strong, but when the weather was nasty, he would sometimes hitch a ride on Poode Eyer's mail truck.

Eyer hauled mail from State College to Tyrone, where he'd pass over the State College mail to postal authorities at the railroad or at the Highway Post Office truck, or HIPO, as locals called it. He'd also pick up any incoming mail earmarked for State College and surrounding communities. Eyer, however, would sometimes carry other cargo as well.

He knew that whenever heavy rains were falling or a driving snowstorm was underway, Sarley Leach would be waiting for him just outside Pine Grove Mills, on the days the mountain hermit needed to go for groceries. The disheveled little man seemed to have an unshakeable faith in the Post Office's unofficial motto: "Neither snow nor rain nor heat nor gloom of night stays these couriers from the swift completion of their appointed rounds." And Eyer, ever true to his employer's credo, never disappointed his regular hitchhiker.

"When he'd take Sarley along, then Sarley would get his groceries," recalled the lifelong resident of Half Moon Valley. "But Sarley would probably hurry, because he also needed to go to the hotel for a little bit," continued our storyteller, who explained that the hotel was where Sarley would go to buy his booze.

"This one time the weather was so bad," said our raconteur, who seemed to have a knack for telling funny stories, "that Poode was late getting into Tyrone. But the other mail was late too, and so he was detained for a while. When he finally did get goin', he went to the grocery store to get Sarley, but Sarley was already gone. So he went to the hotel, and that's where Sarley was.

"And so he said, 'Come on Sarley, the weather's bad and it's gettin' colder, and we gotta get headed home."

"So Sarley said, 'All right', and Poode went out to wait for him."

"Then he come out and got in, and they were drivin' along. It was rough goin', but they got into Warriors Mark and headed for Seven Stars. But just as they were goin' up over Mile Hill there, why Sarley says 'Poode, you gotta stop! I gotta take a leak!'

"Poode said, 'Well I'm not stoppin' here in the middle of this hill. Wait until we get to the top!'

"Sarley said, 'Well hurry Poode, will ya!'

"So Poode said, 'Well, I'll hurry.'

"They got to the top of the hill, and Poode stopped and said, 'There Sarley, go ahead and let her run!'

"So Sarley got out, and it was takin' him awhile, and Poode wondered why. So Poode pulled a banana out of his dinner box, thinkin' he'd eat it while he was waiting. He had just started to unpeel it when Sarley opened the door.

"It was howlin' and blowin', and Sarley says 'Poode, you gotta get out and help me! I can't find it!'

So Poode got out and walked around the front of the truck, and when he got over to Sarley he asked him 'What's the matter?'

'Well, I can't find it!' came the plaintive response.

"He had three or four pair of pants on, and he was too drunk to get 'em all unbuttoned," explained our entertaining source.

"So Poode started to unbutton one or two pair, and he still wasn't clear. He was tired of unbuttoning, and so he just shoved that banana in there.

"And he says, 'There it is Sarley, let her run!'

"So Sarley said, "Okay Poode. Thanks."

"And so he stood there a little bit, and Poode said, 'Aren't you gonna hurry up; it's gettin' cold here! When you're done, shake it off and let's get outa here!'

"Well, Poode said when Sarley shook it, the end broke off, and he said to Sarley 'My God, Sarley, you broke it off!'

"'Yes, I know,' came the faint reply that was tinged with an unmistaken tone of terror, 'and I feel the blood runnin' down my leg!'"[1]

MINK DAWSON'S LAST DRINK

(Setting: the 1950s in the Black Horse Tavern, Reedsville, Mifflin County. I've changed the last name of the family slightly so as not to offend anyone.)

Back in the wildest parts of New Lancaster Valley, where Thick Mountain and Jacks Mountain butt up against one another to form Reeds Gap State Park in the western end of the valley, and Snyder Middleswarth State Park in the eastern end, few settlements can be found in old New Lancaster even today. Only scattered residences and hunting camps dot the landscape through this section; but fifty years ago, it was even less densely populated.

Among the more prominent and more numerous families residing here at that time were the Dawsons; a clan known, deservedly or not, for their hard drinking; moral standards that left much to be desired; and territoriality. Although it was well known that the Dawsons regularly violated state game laws, only the bravest game wardens dared question them about it. Those that did were roughed up and escorted out of the valley, with a warning not to come back.

It seemed that, to a man, the Dawsons were a fearless and bold lot to deal with, but it is said that the toughest one of all was "Mink." No one today seems to know how he got that nickname, but his reputation as a rough and tumble ridge-runner has survived. One of the tales told about him was how Mink was frustrated over his and his relatives' inability to bag a nice big buck that was often seen in the valley. Vowing to down it himself, the hardy hill hawk set off one day with only his hunting knife in hand. After a short trek through the woods, Dawson climbed a tree standing beside the path the deer was known to travel, and, after concealing himself in the leaves, settled in to await a final showdown.

His patience was soon rewarded, and as the big deer passed underneath, Mink threw himself down on its back. He struggled to get a good grip on the crazed animal's neck, hoping to free one hand so he could use his knife to slit the deer's throat. It was an even struggle for a while, but

---

1. Joseph Fye (born 1940), recorded February 24, 2004.

Precursor to today's lie detector. At least that's what could
be said if the old story is true that a setup like this was once
used to catch a chicken thief in the Tuscarora Mountains of
Perry County. (Picture drawn by James J. Frazier.)

eventually it was the deer, not the determined hunter, that got the upper hand. In fact, the hunter may have taken some of the battle scars from that fight to his grave.

When Mink died, some years later, his family took his body to the Bohn Funeral Home (still in business today) in Reedsville. Some days later, after the body had been laid out and was ready for burial, Mink's brothers, perhaps in a state of inebriation themselves, decided that Mink needed one more drink before he was "planted." All of the brothers, to a man, thought that one last glass of brew with their dead kinsman would afford them some real monkeyshines, until one of them asked how they would get Mink's body.

Certainly the funeral home was not going to give it to them without proper legal permission, and it was not likely that the authorities would approve such a plan anyway. There the matter stood for a while until one of the men proposed that they just sneak the body out of the Bohn's funeral hall that night, and then sneak it back after Mink had his drink, so no one would be the wiser.

That night the men were able to execute the first part of their plan without a hitch, managing to get Mink out of the Bohn funeral establishment and into the Black Horse. Once into the tavern, the brothers carried Mink over to the bar and propped him up on a stool. Each and every patron in the place looked on in amazement, some perhaps vowing to stop imbibing then and there if this was the kind of *delirium tremens* their regular drinking was starting to cause.

Seemingly oblivious to the sensation they had created, the Dawson brothers ordered a drink for the dead man. It is said that at this point the bar "cleared out in a hurry" and that the bartender "wanted to get out in the worst kind of way too!" Whether Mink ever got his drink or not is not recalled, but the police finally came and took him back to the funeral home. As for his brothers, they might have been taken somewhere else for the night.[2]

TO CATCH A THIEF
(Setting: late 1800s or early 1900s in the Pine Grove/Jericho area of Perry County)
Similar to the old adage that "there's more than one way to skin a cat," there were many ways people used to think a thief could be brought to justice as well. Among the strangest of these was the procedure prescribed by John George Hohman, the great witch doctor of the Blue Mountains. *Pow-wows or His Long Lost Friend, Mysterious Arts and Remedies for Man as well as Animals*, published in Reading around 1820, was the Powwower's desk reference guide during the nineteenth and early twentieth century. Containing many diverse "cures," charms, and spells, the small booklet was guaranteed to help the common man protect himself from diseases, witches, and the devil himself.

Satan's henchmen, including the common thief, were not exempt from the powerful spells included in Hohman's arsenal of incantations either; and compelling a malefactor to return stolen goods was said to be easily accomplished. The tricky part, however, was finding the skull of another thief and locating a supple juniper.

---

2. Craig Weidensaul, interviewed by telephone February 24, 2001.

Once the necessary items were located, the only thing the person who had been robbed needed to do was to take the skull and walk out to the juniper "in the early morning before sunrise." Then the tree was to be bent "with the left hand toward the rising sun." While doing this the person was to recite: "Juniper tree I shall bend and squeeze thee until the thief has returned the stolen goods to the place from which he took them!"

When the leafy top of the tree was bent to the ground, the skull was to be placed under the leaves, and a stone, heavy enough to keep the tree from springing back to its upright position, was then placed on the treetop. The only precaution suggested by Hohman to those with nerve enough to carry out his ceremony was that "you must be careful, in case the thief returns the stolen goods, to unloose the bush and replace the stone to where it was before!"[3]

For those without the courage to follow Hohman's guidelines, there were alternative ways that could be used to catch the person who enjoyed taking things that didn't belong to them. However, even in some of these cases the procedures could prove stressful to those who used them, or so a man who lived near Spring Mills in Centre County found out one day when braucher Bennie Ripka told him how to get his stolen hams back.

Bennie told Jerry Corman that one of his neighbors had taken the fresh hams when the man had been helping at Uncle Jerry's butchering.

"You go to the festival [today we'd call them a carnival] in town tonight," Bennie advised Uncle Jerry, "and every neighbor you come across, you look straight in the eye, because the thief won't be able to break eye contact!" So, the theft victim went to the evening's festivities, and when he saw one of his neighbors, he looked him straight in the eye, just like the old braucher had told him to do.

According to those who had heard the rest of the story, the neighbor started to shake and shiver, and try as he might, he couldn't break eye contact with Uncle Jerry. Finally, Jerry Corman broke the eye contact on his own because, noted Corman's great niece, "He figured he was the one who took his hams, and he said if he kept looking him in the eye, he figured it would have killed him!"[4]

Not all thief-revealing charms were as life threatening or as gruesome as those mentioned so far; at least according to this tale I collected in Perry

3. John George Hohman, *Pow-wows, or the Long Lost Friend*, 62.
4. Nedra Meyer, recorded June 6, 1999.

County. Somewhere in the foothills of the Tuscarora Mountains of Perry County, near the small towns of Jericho and Pine Grove, there was once another farmer who, during the 1890s, was also the victim of a robbery. The Perry County husbandman suspected a neighbor of stealing one of his chickens, but he wasn't sure how to bring him to justice. He finally decided to talk to his preacher, who affably agreed to help him out.

"You invite the suspect and four other neighbors to your farm," advised the clergyman, "and before they arrive, take one of your big old black butchering kettles and turn it upside down in your yard."

On the day the five neighbors arrived at the farm, the preacher was there too, "for moral support," and to conduct the proceedings. After having the men gather around the kettle, the "sky pilot," the name some of the non-churchmen liked to use when referring to the minister, explained to the five neighbors that someone had stolen the farmer's chicken, and they were there to help find out who it was.

The solemn preacher went on to explain that there was a rooster under the kettle, and he noted that each man was to pass by the kettle and run their right hand over it several times as they passed. The rooster would, said the dour cleric, crow when the guilty man touched the pot.

With that said, the five men took their turns rubbing the butcher kettle, and after all had done so, without a sound from the rooster, the minister had them all put their right hand out in front of them with palm up. Five hands appeared in near unison, and while four of the palms were covered with black soot; the fifth man's hand was clean. "There's your thief," the minister expostulated, as he tipped over the kettle to show there was no rooster under it after all.[5]

The clever preacher had put black soot all over the bottom of the kettle, thinking that the guilty man would probably be afraid to rub it, only pretending to do so when he passed his hand over it. The reverend had also counted on the hope that the men all knew about and believed in the ancient idea that the cock could be used as a potent instrument in the subjugation of evil spirits. It was a notion once held by many English peasants of Lancashire, and also a flourish that Hindoo mystics once incorporated in their rites of exorcism.[6]

5. Merle Varner (born 1906), recorded January 11, 1985.
6. Charles Hardwick, *Traditions, Superstitions, and Folk-lore*, 137–38.

IN SICKNESS AND IN HEALTH
(Setting: late 1880s in Centre Hall, Centre County)

Among the many hardships endured by the state's earliest settlers was a scarcity of doctors, and one incident that typifies that dearth of medical practitioners occurred in Harford Township of Susquehanna County during the late 1700s. Around that time, Mrs. Mercy Tyler was a veritable Florence Nightingale for the region's settlers. Not trained as a doctor, she would nonetheless "ride on horseback for miles around to visit the sick."[7]

But despite her diligence, Mrs. Tyler was sometimes storm-stayed, and one winter day the snow was so deep that Mrs. Tyler could not make her rounds. However, one nearby resident was deathly ill, and her relatives had such faith in Mrs. Tyler's skills that four sturdy men volunteered to bring her to the patient on their shoulders.

It is recalled that the men did exactly that. After strapping on their snowshoes, they waded through the deep drifts between the sick woman's house and Mrs. Tyler's residence. When they got there, they wrapped the good woman in a blanket, hoisted her onto their shoulders, and carried her back to the waiting patient.[8]

If the experiences of Seth Nelson's family were typical of the times, it would seem that the early settlers of Northumberland County often had to fend for themselves when incapacitated by illness. The Nelsons settled around Watsontown, Northumberland County, about 1812 when Seth was just two years old. In addition to a scarcity of money during that period, there was a scarcity of physicians, and according to an early sketch of the old man's life, the family was plagued by much illness during their stay at Watsontown. In fact, the old man recalled that at times "everyone in the family was so ill they could not attend to each other's wants."[9]

Victims of diseases in those early days could often only endure them. The scarcity of doctors and lack of miracle drugs that afforded relief from pain and misery meant people had to "tough it out" as best they could, and judging from the descriptions of the illnesses that made the rounds in those days, death must have seemed a welcome alternative to those suffering from plagues with names like black measles, rotten throat, flux, wildfire,

7. Emily C. Blackman, *History of Susquehanna County, Pennsylvania*, 183.
8. Ibid.
9. Rose Nelson (daughter), biography of Seth Nelson, 1890s. Copy provided to author by Mrs. R. B. Caskey of Renovo.

and other such nasty-sounding ailments. Little wonder, then, that people turned to their own devices and even sometimes resorted to supernatural means for countering sickness.

Beliefs that certain winds carried diseases, or that *en hex muss immer ebber gwele* (a witch who has given herself into the power of the devil is compelled to continually torment people) were widely held at one time; and revealed a believer's penchant for relying upon superstitions as much as upon doctors or herbal remedies like *chonni hossensack* (dutchman's breeches), bergamot, white baneberry, and sassafras for their medical needs.

One other clue as to whether a person's medical beliefs tended toward the supernatural was the name they gave to their dog. It was not uncommon to find, during those early times, that many dogs were named Wasser. The basis for that name, which means water when translated from the Pennsylvania Dutch, was that it was well known that witches had a phobia for water. It was therefore thought that by naming your dog after the liquid witch repellent, witches would be too afraid to cast spells upon your household.[10]

One hundred or more years later, in the late 1890s, attitudes had changed, as had the supply of doctors and their arsenal of drugs for combating illness. Nonetheless, there were many of the old diseases that still survived and do so to this day, including several of the sexually transmitted variety.

From 1877 through 1890, W. A. Jacobs served as the physician for the small town of Centre Hall in Centre County. Doc Jacobs, as he was referred to by most of the townspeople, was never at a loss for patients, as his clientele not only included the town folk but the people living in adjoining Potter Township as well.

The good doctor was called upon to treat all varieties of illness, including venereal diseases like genital herpes, syphilis, and gonorrhea, which in those days, and today also for that matter, was referred to in vulgar terms as the clap.

One day a man came into Jacobs' office and asked for a consultation. Upon sitting down with the doctor, the visitor stated that he had a friend "who thinks he has the clap."

10. Fredric Klees, *The Pennsylvania Dutch*, 305; Thomas R. Brendle and Charles W. Unger, *Folk Medicine of the Pennsylvania Germans*, 208.

"What should he do," queried the Good Samaritan, in an apparent gesture of kindness.

Doctor Jacobs, perhaps because he knew the man or because this was not the first time he had encountered embarrassed patients in similar situations, was not fooled.

"Well, haul out your *friend* and let's have a look," was the reply of the country doctor, who, like many of his old-time predecessors, knew how to diagnose and comfort their patients by relying upon hard-won years of on-the-job experience, common sense, and a reassuring bedside manner.[11]

FRUGALITY

(Setting: The 1940s, Somewhere in the Pennsylvania Dutch countryside)

Jokes about the proverbial stingy Scotchman have made the rounds for ages, but the early settlers of Pennsylvania also had to be tight with a dollar in order to just survive. In fact, life then could be so hard that even the last morsel of food was considered a precious commodity.

"Me and the woman came out on foot, driving one little cow and carrying all our effects on our backs," wrote one Venango County settler when describing his entry into northwestern Pennsylvania.

"The first year we ate potatoes and slept on leaves. The first wheat I raised I took a bushel on my back, walked to Pittsburgh, got it ground and carried back the flour. Seed was so scarce that on one occasion when a hen had eaten some melon seeds placed in the sun to dry, the owner cut open the chicken's crop, extracted the seeds, and then sewed up the gash because she couldn't afford to lose either the seeds or the hen. The hen recovered"![12]

Similar to the proverbial stingy Scotchman, or to the early settlers of Venango County, the Pennsylvania Amish man has gained a reputation for thrift and frugality. The Amish sect has managed to preserve their way of life so that it differs very little from what it was centuries ago. It is, perhaps, for this reason that they are also famous for their thrifty and savings ways, seemingly as careful with their money today as the pioneer settlers of Venango County were 300 years ago. Little wonder, then, that jokes about thrifty Amish men have surfaced from time to time, just like jokes about thrifty Scotchmen.

---

11. Robert F. Frazier (born 1920), recorded October 31, 1997.
12. Stevenson W. Fletcher, *Pennsylvania Agriculture and Country Life, 1640–1840*, 78.

One such humorous tale has found its way to different parts of Pennsylvania, with milk jugs being the place where the Amish man stored his money, according to the Tioga County version of the tale. In Centre County, "An Amish couple went to buy a farm, and after they had agreed upon the price and everything, why, the Amish man sent his young son out to get a shoebox with money in it," recalled my father. "And the son went out and got the shoebox and come back in. There was $20,000 in the box, and the Amish man gave his son the dickens, saying 'you got the wrong box!'

"He was supposed to go out and get the one with the 50- or 80,000 in it"![13]

---

13. Robert F. Frazier (born 1920), recorded December 13, 1988; James Y. Glimm, *Flatlanders and Ridgerunners*, 36.

CHAPTER 8

PHANTOMS OF THE FOREST

Given its stealthy nocturnal habits and its uncanny ability to avoid contact with humans, the wolf might aptly be referred to as a phantom of the forest. This elusive trait was one that proved to be particularly frustrating to early Pennsylvania's trappers, who found wolves almost impossible to catch in one of their steel traps. Time and time again upon checking their trap lines they would find the traps set for wolves had been sprung.

Over time the savvy wolves had apparently learned how to detect concealed traps, spring them, and walk off with the appetizing bait as their reward. It was an occurrence that happened so often that the trappers started to refer to wolves as "shadows of the forest."[1] It was almost as though the trappers wanted to convey the notion that wolves had some supernatural qualities that made them so hard to trap, which in turn would mean the cause wasn't the trappers' poor trapping skills!

Mountain lions too, possessing the same elusive and secretive qualities as the wolf, could just as easily be considered for the same title as well. Once thought to be extinct here in the Keystone State, *Felis concolor*, as biologists refer to it, seems to be making a comeback of sorts. Sightings of huge cats, thought by many to be mountain lions, have increased dramatically in the Pennsylvania mountains in recent years, almost as though the wily beasts had only been in hiding for over a hundred years and have just now decided to make a reappearance.

---

1. E. N. Woodcock, *Fifty Years a Hunter and Trapper*, 11.

As noted in previous chapters in this series, the Pennsylvania mountain lion population declined dramatically following the Civil War until their unsettling call of the wild was finally heard no more in the state's mountains, foothills, hollows, and valleys. In fact, if it weren't for the many nerve-racking encounters with the beasts that those living amongst them once had, memories of the big cats, referred to as panthers and in various other ways by the early settlers, might have died away as swiftly as the panther did.

However, because those early settlers did have some close calls when attacked by mountain lions, accounts about the one-time presence of the panther in Pennsylvania's hills is preserved forever in local historical records, in volumes of wildlife or natural history, and in the oral history of some parts of the state where the old tales have lingered the longest. Following are some of those old panther tales that I was fortunate enough to save at the final hour before they too disappeared. However, unlike the wily panther, which may indeed have found its way back into our hills, the disappearance of the following tales would have been irreversible; they would not have found their way back from oblivion.

THE PHANTOM PANTHER

This account was told to me one fine June afternoon, in an isolated mountain home that sits along the little-traveled dirt mountain road called the Millheim-Siglerville Pike. It was an appropriate place to hear a tale of the long ago, and that, plus the story itself, made us want to travel through some relatively unspoiled parts of the nearby mountains.

Consequently, after hearing the narrative of the phantom panther, we decided we'd follow the old pike into the wilds of the Stillhouse Hollow and over to the isolated beauty of the Big Poe Mountain country. The drive was a pleasant one, especially after hearing a panther tale. However, the place where the incident with the phantom panther occurred was somewhere in the mountains above Georges Valley in Centre County. The time period when it supposedly took place was sometime in the 1890s, and the man who encountered the strange animal was the storyteller's grandfather.

The old gentleman apparently had heard about a lost treasure trove in the area that dated back to the time of the Revolutionary War. He also seemed to be convinced that there was more to the panther he encountered that day than met the eye, because after he struck it, the big cat just silently disappeared into the woods without as much as giving his assailant another look.

"My grandfather was a Braught," began our hostess, who knew many tales of the type we liked to hear and collect. "He always walked on the mountain," she continued. He also always carried a cane with him because he wanted to make sure there were no snakes lying around. One time he came across this animal, he said it was a panther, and he struck it with his cane to get it out of his way.

"Well, the cane bounced off the cat and snapped him on the calf of his one leg so hard that it later got infected. I remember the wound on his leg; it seeped and stayed infected for the rest of his life"!

Whether the old man just never went to get medicine for his injury or whether it was one of those that didn't respond to the medicines of that day we'll never know. However, the superstitious mountaineer took the stubborn wound as a sign that he had missed out on finding a fortune.

"He swore," concluded our storyteller, "that if he'd have talked to the critter instead of hitting it, it would have turned into a man, dressed in a suit of clothes from the Revolutionary days, who could've taken him to some gold!"[2]

TROUBLE FROM ABOVE

Panthers were not usually regarded, as in the last tale, as links to lost treasure. However, they were known for their affinity for trees, both as a safe haven and as a place of attack. In describing the habits of the panther, Clinton County pioneer Philip Tome noted that "it moves in tremendous bounds, but it can maintain this movement but a short time, soon becoming fatigued and ascending a tree."[3]

Mountaineers from Tome's time, and even up into the late 1800s, would probably have confirmed Tome's statements, just like the man who was jumped by a treed panther near where Immel Road enters Poe Valley State Park, Centre County, sometime between 1850 and 1870. The panther missed its mark, and its intended victim lived to tell the tale to his son, who in turn told it to me. The account provides a glimpse into what

2. Nedra Meyer, recorded June 6, 1999.
3. Philip Tome, *Pioneer Life or Thirty Years a Hunter*, 111.

dangers lurked in the trees of the forest of an earlier day. Indeed, it can be said that during those times people did truly experience "trouble from above."

"My dad was jumped by a panther in Poe Valley," said the eighty-seven-year-old teller of the old tales. "It missed him and landed behind him. Panthers, once on the ground, won't jump at you again if they missed their jump from a tree, but they'll get ahead of you and try to jump you from above again. Dad had a pistol with him, and he just kept firing it all the way home. He could hear the panther, but the shots seemed to scare it off so that it didn't try to jump him again."[4]

Sometime during the first several decades following the Civil War, there was another panther lying in wait in the limbs of a tree that stood along the roadway still known today as the Millheim Narrows. This unsettled section of forest, where Brush and Shriner Mountains come together to form many little hollows and even smaller "kettles," is where Elk Creek winds its way northward from Penn's Valley into neighboring Brush Valley. If there is any place in Pennsylvania where a panther might be found today, it is here.

During the late 1940s a panther was seen near the old stone watering trough that sat beside the Millheim Narrows road. It was once a well-used stopping place for wagoners passing through the Narrows. Here they would stop to water their teams of horses that pulled wagons filled with loads of hemlock bark destined for local tanneries via the railroad siding in Coburn.

Even as recently as the late 1970s there was a stir created in the area when someone claimed they saw a panther up on Shriner Mountain. Since that time there have been no sightings of panthers in this section of the county, and even the heavy stone trough, a notable Millheim Narrows landmark, has disappeared, stolen by selfish miscreants sometime after 1971.

Fortunately, however, some of the tales from the Narrows' early times cannot be stolen away as long as there are people who appreciate them and pass them on to their descendants. One such story is that of Charles Grimes' panther, and how it jumped upon him from the leafy branches of a tree where it had concealed itself one day.

Grimes lived in the Narrows, in a home owned most recently by a family named Foringher. Early one morning Grimes walked out into Brush Valley to help at a butchering, and when he returned later that afternoon,

---

4. Ralph Lingle (born 1900), recorded August 27, 1972.

he was carrying sausages he had been given for his help. As he passed under the tree where the panther lay in waiting, the tired farmer didn't have any warning before the big cat jumped down upon him. The beast didn't land right on its victim, but it hit him hard enough that it caused him to drop the sausages he was carrying.

The cat immediately pounced on the sausage meat, which is what it smelled in the first place, and that gave Grimes enough time to escape. Running home as fast as he could, the lucky man, when he got there, grabbed his rifle. He and his two sons, both of whom brought their rifles as well, returned to the place where he had been attacked. There they found the panther calmly feasting on the sausage meat it had just so brazenly stolen. The large animal was enjoying its meal so much that it did not notice the three men take up positions around it. It paid for its carelessness with its life.

The Grimes family skinned the panther and had the hide tanned. They passed it on to their grandchildren, who in turn passed it on to theirs. Thus, it was kept in the family for years as a valued souvenir of the fearful creature that once almost claimed the life of the family patriarch during those times when panthers were not uncommon in the Millheim Narrows.

However, just like the watering trough, the panther hide has also disappeared over the years, its whereabouts unknown. Both items would today be unique links to the past and lingering reminders of those early days of horses, wagons, and the big cats that would sometimes drop unexpectedly from the trees above.[5]

THE DORMAN PANTHER

This tale provides an old-time example of how panthers will take to the trees when threatened. It is an account, preserved through several generations of Louis Dorman's descendants, telling how Dorman killed what was probably the last panther in this section of Centre County. The Dorman homestead, standing west of Fox's Gap along Shriner Mountain, Centre County, is still used as a home today. The barn here is a new one; the original structure where the panther spent the night was not very large and burned down decades ago. Louis Dorman was born June 10, 1820; he is buried in Saint Paul's Union Cemetery, below Woodward. He died November 28, 1905.

---

5. Clarence Musser (born 1884), interviewed August 28, 1971, and November 12, 1971.

Dorman's account came down to the present day from Louis himself, who passed it on to his son Davy, who then told it to his son Howard, who in turn entertained my informant's grandparents with the tale; they then one day recalled the same story to my informant when he was a young lad.

The panther appears to have grown over-confident. It had stolen several of "Louie" Dorman's pigs; then one night it decided to sleep in Dorman's barn. During that night a good tracking snow blew in (it was the month of December), and when Dorman saw the panther's tracks leading out of his barn very early the next morning, almost, as they still say in the mountains, "at the crack of dawn," he decided he would follow the thieving monster.

"He had a dog which would trail," recalled our interesting link to the past, "and he started to trail the panther on the west side of Fox's Gap. He took it up over the gap knob, and part way out on the sun side (This is an old-time term for the south side of a mountain—JRF) of old Shriner Mountain. And out close to Hosterman's Gap it came down on the sun side again. Then he trailed it east to slightly beyond where the bridge crosses Pine Creek. A little bit east of that bridge and about fifty yards off the road is where Louie got the first shot.

"Now this was with an old muzzleloader I imagine. The dog had treed the panther, and he got a shot in, but he didn't kill it. It came down out of the tree, and he trailed it another three miles out Pine Creek Hollow to where the Danville Camp is today. Here, at the spring, he killed the panther. So 'til he had it skinned, it was a long day I imagine!

"My grandmother Motz, she was Thomas Hosterman's daughter, was born eight years after this, but remembered her parents telling her that Dorman came to their farmhouse there in Hosterman's Gap after shooting the panther and held the dead animal's head up to their window and scared them!"[6]

HOW TO HANDLE A PANTHER
Around 1895, Solomon Wise was visiting his friends the Orndorfs, who lived about a quarter mile away from his blacksmith shop in Brush Valley, Centre County. Wise had the physique that most people mentally visualize as a big, burly, village blacksmith; and not much seemed to intimidate him. At least, when he saw a large tawny panther on the road in front of him

---

6. Randall Stover (born 1919), recorded September 25, 1999.

Mrs. Ida Hosterman Motz. Born in 1865, eight years after Louis Dorman shot his panther on Shriner Mountain in Centre County, Mrs. Motz was fond of recalling how Dorman scared her parents by holding the dead panther's head up to their window. The old lady also had personally known Hairy John Voneida, the "hermit of the narrows." See the author's Volume III and the chapter entitled "Hairy John" to find out more about this unusual character. This photo of Mrs. Motz, taken in 1953 when she was 88, appears in the Haines Township Bicentennial Committee publication entitled Haines Township Life and Tradition Centre County Pennsylvania, published in 1976.

when walking over to Orndorfs, he didn't back down. First, he hollered at it, then continued to do so while running right at it. The bold feint worked, and the panther ran away. Whenever Wise would tell this story, even in his later years, it is recalled he would always conclude by sagely noting "and that's the only way to handle them panthers!"[7]

There were others, however, who would have taken exception to Sol Wise's proclamations, including a new Irish immigrant who lived near Milesburg, Centre County, during the late 1700s. At that time, it was still not uncommon for panthers to attack a farmer's livestock, and some painters, as they were sometimes called, seemed to have developed a fondness for pigs.

One night a hog in Andrew Boggs' pigsty was carried off by a panther, and the next night the Irishman, who was working as Boggs' hired man,

7. Clarence Musser, Ibid.

was assigned guard duty with the instructions to sound an alarm if the panther appeared on the scene again. Shortly after everyone else had retired for the night, the Irishman heard the pigs begin to squeal.

Seeing the panther running away with the pig in its possession, he gave chase and tackled it. He managed to grab some large stones and sticks; and used those as clubs with some effect, until the panther got loose and then pounced at him. Fortunately, the feisty Irishman had procured a large cudgel with which to defend himself, and when the panther made its attack, it was knocked senseless from a well-directed blow on the head.

By this time Mr. Boggs, awakened by the commotion, arrived on the scene only to discover a large panther lying dead at the Irishman's feet. When he explained to the man what danger he had just encountered and what the animal was that he had just killed, it is recalled that the Irishman made a "beeline" for the house, and "never afterwards was known to be out after dark without someone to accompany him."[8]

Most men would not have been as brave as Andrew Boggs' Irishman, but one Irishwoman came close. Up in Luzerne County, near the small village of Alden, there was once, sometime during those times when panthers were on the wane in this part of the state, a woman who lived in a shack on Alden Mountain. Her name was Mrs. Finn, and she was remembered by my storyteller as "a typical Irish woman, with one tooth, scraggly white hair, and a wrinkled face with skin that looked like old leather." She was also a self-reliant, tough, old lady, and even when "up in her eighties" would regularly walk all the way down the mountain to Jake Fine's general store in Alden.

Jake Fine, it is recalled, was "a typical witty country storekeeper, with a white handlebar mustache and always in need of a haircut." One morning Mrs. Finn came into Jake's store with a box of new matches she had bought there, saying that this morning when she tried to light her fire, she couldn't get a single one of them to light. The matches were the type known as barnburners. They were designed to ignite easily when rubbed on almost any surface, and so the old storekeeper took one and rubbed it across the seat of his corduroy pants, and it lit right up.

Mrs. Finn, somewhat perplexed by the ease with which Jake Fine had lit the match, took her box and went back up the mountain. When she got

---

8. John Blair Linn, *History of Centre and Clinton Counties*, 261.

home, she tried to light one of her matches, and again had no success. So once more she went down the mountain to Jake Fine, and again he lit one of her matches on the back of his pants.

"Jake Fine," expostulated Mrs. Finn, "if you think I'm gonna walk five miles down the mountain to light a match on your ass every time I want a fire, you're crazy!"

This little anecdote was recalled here just to give the reader an idea of how tough and determined the old lady was, because one morning in her woodshed she would need all the grit and determination she could muster. About a hundred feet from her shack on the mountain, Mrs. Finn had a woodshed where she kept her firewood.

Bright and early one winter morning she went out to get an armload of her wood for her morning fire, just like she did every day. However, on this day when she opened the door, she spied an enormous panther lying on top of her woodpile. But instead of backing off and running for the safety of her home, the old woman grabbed a sturdy piece of wood and, with one smashing blow, knocked out the mountain lion. She then proceeded to club it to death. The beast, it is recalled, was one of the last, if not the last, panthers killed in the Wyoming Valley.[9]

KEEPING THEM AT BAY
Beside the methods noted in the tales above, and also in other chapters of previous volumes in this series, there were at least two other notable ways that people found to be effective when trying to discourage a hungry panther that seemed to be considering them as a meal.

During one of my book signings, a lady mentioned to me that her grandmother had once been followed by a panther, somewhere in either Clinton or Lycoming County. The lady disappeared before I could get her grandmother's name or other details, but the story stuck in my mind because of its uniqueness.

The young girl in danger must have been terrified, but she kept her presence of mind. Instead of running away, which she knew would be futile, she somehow came up with the idea to start tearing off pieces of her dress and throwing them on the road behind her as she went along.

9. W. G. Jones (born 1905), interviewed February 2, 1974.

Apparently, the panther would stop at each piece and sniff at it to determine what it was.

The ploy gave the young lady enough leeway between herself and the panther that she managed to get home safely. Sadly, the young heroine's name will never be known since the lady who told me the tale didn't stay long enough for me to get, as news commentator Paul Harvey is fond of saying, "the rest of the story." If the lady reads this, I would appreciate it if she would get in touch.

Unfortunately, names have also been lost over time of two young men who had a similar panther scare while walking through a lonely and wild hollow of the Allegheny Mountains during the early 1900s. Fortunately the story of their encounter, and the unique way they fended off the panther that was stalking them, has managed to survive down to the present time.

During the first several decades of the twentieth century, a family named Kline ran a stave mill operation below the main chain of the Allegheny Mountains in Blair County. It was not unusual for the lumber mill to turn out four to five thousand chestnut staves a day; and with such a big operation, there were hired hands who helped with the work. It was not unusual for the men to wear out their canvas gloves in a matter of days as a result of handling so many wooden staves on a daily basis.

So it was that late one afternoon in 1911, after a hard day's work at the Kline stave mill, two of the Klines' hired hands were sent into the nearby town of Bald Eagle to purchase a gross of new canvas gloves. It was a fairly long walk, out through California Hollow, and by the time the young men arrived at the feed mill store in town, made their purchase, and started back through the hollow, it was turning dark.

"Well, anyways," said our storyteller, who remembered that night as vividly as though it had happened just last week, "when they were comin' back, this panther, they used to call them painters, started to holler right close to them! And they didn't have no flashlight, and so they started to burn the gloves. I don't know how many they burnt before they got back, but they were all excited when they told us the story."

Although the burning gloves kept the bold panther at bay and allowed the two young lumbermen to reach safety, their technique didn't scare the painter off entirely. Apparently, it remained in the area that evening, arousing the protective sense of the Klines' dogs; because, noted our link with the old days, the animals "raised the devil that night," somehow sensing the presence of the big cat.[10]

GONE, BUT NOT FORGOTTEN

Among the hunting tales passed on to us by the man who told us the last story, was an account about a panther his great uncle, Jacob Long, shot somewhere along Brush Mountain of Centre County about 1910. The old Brush Valley farmer had a dog that was apparently rather talented in sniffing out big game.

He'd let his dog out occasionally to see what it would scare up; and whenever he'd hear it barking, he knew that it had probably treed a panther or was on its track. Long would then follow the sound of the barking until he found his dog, and if it had treed a panther, he would shoot the big beast out of its hiding place.

"He shot one one morning," recollected our interesting raconteur, "and he had it layin' there in his barnyard. He hadn't skinned it yet, but he had two or three panther hides tacked up on his barn. There was a doctor that come there that morning, and he seen this panther layin' there, and he said, 'Oh, give me that panther. I'll take it home and have it mounted.'

"So he gave him the panther, and they had it there in the museum down in Harrisburg. I took the kids down there from school—we used to have the buses—and I asked them where the panther was. 'Oh,' they said, 'we got rid of it. It got real crummy!'"

It was a disappointing ending to the panther story, and it had been a disappointment to our storyteller when he had discovered that the panther hide had been destroyed. However, the memory of the panther lived on in his mind until he died, and now it will live on a while longer now that the story he passed on to me and has been recorded in this book.[11]

NOTE TO THE TALES: As indicated at the beginning of this chapter, panther sightings have begun to increase in recent years, or at least some people think so, and the sightings come from reputable individuals who know that what they saw was something out of the ordinary. Nonetheless,

10. Royal Kline (born 1901), recorded January 2, 2000.
11. Ibid.

they still have trouble convincing their friends of that fact, just like the man who saw two big cats in Poe Valley State Park about 25 years ago.

About that time, Al Harpster and his wife were living along Poe Run, near Poe Valley State Park. The Harpsters lived there year-round, and both loved the solitude and beauty of their forest home. Al, a true mountain man, enjoyed hunting as one of his favorite pastimes, and one night he decided to go "spotting" for deer. "He was tellin' me this, and said he'd gone spotting a night or so before, and he saw a panther" noted the man who was telling me the story that Harpster had told to him. "So, his friends over in Lewistown said, 'Now Al, you've got to stay away from the booze!'

"He said, 'No, I wasn't drinkin' any booze!'

"They said, 'Al you must've been drunk, because there's no panthers around!'

"So they came in a week or so later, and they went spotting. And on up the road there was two—a tan one and a darker-phased one. And the guy says, 'Al! Wha, wha, wha, what the hell is that!'

"He said, 'That's the last beer you drank!' And this was right down there in Poe Valley!"[12]

12. Randall Stover, Ibid.

CHAPTER 9

FACES FROM THE PAST

It has been said that the mountains of Pennsylvania "brood upon things eternal."[1] Whoever made that statement could have been thinking at the time of how many dark hollows, fog-laden glens, and mist-shrouded valleys exist in the Pennsylvania hills, and perhaps they fell into a contemplative mood themselves. Then maybe they went a step further and thought such a mood seemed a fitting one to attribute to the somber and silent mountains that sometimes seem lofty enough to be constantly engaged in higher thoughts, in continuous communion with the gods. On the other hand, the person who viewed our mountains as brooding might have had something else in mind. Perhaps they were thinking of the rock profiles that were once celebrated as the visages of some of Pennsylvania's Indian chiefs.

There were at one time several such natural rock profiles that adorned the cliffs of different peaks in the Keystone State, but whether or not they still can be seen today is doubtful. Unremitting road construction crews have given little thought to such natural wonders when carving away whole sides of mountains to expand the roadway system which continues to grow like a malignancy; and Mother Nature is no better. Unrelenting natural forces and weathering finally caused the famous "Old Man of the Mountain" profile in New Hampshire to break away from its cliff-side perch in recent years, and a similar fate might have befallen Pennsylvania's rock profiles. The prospect of one's demise is certainly something to cause melancholia if it is dwelt upon, but the bleak interpretation ascribed to

1. C. A. Higgins, *Titans of Chasms*, 10.

the feelings nature may have tried to capture when fashioning the rock visages of Pennsylvania's Indian chiefs might be attributable to other reasons as well.

One such alternate example would have to be the rock profile of Delaware Indian chief Lapachpeton, still clinging to a rock cliff that sits along the Susquehanna River one mile south of Danville, Montour County (see picture at the front of this book). The old chief's village was located at the mouth of Catawissa Creek, probably on or near the present site of the town of Catawissa in Columbia County. Here the great man was held in high esteem by the Delaware and Conoy peoples whom he led, and he was also known as a friend to the settlers. Not much else seems to be known about him today, so aside from his small place in the history books, his hold on immortality depended solely on the durability of his rock profile and on the mournful story of his daughter Minnetunke.

Minnetunke's story is a common one, at least as far as tales of star-crossed Indian maidens go. In fact, it has been suggested that if Indian lovers' suicides actually occurred at every place in Pennsylvania where a legend says they did, then the practice must have had a significant effect on the Indian population of the state. The statement is an exaggeration, of course, but it does point out the fact that the tale of Indian lovers committing suicide is a widespread and common one. Each tale has its own variation, but the basic story is always the same, just like in the legend of Minnetunke (see the author's story entitled "Maids of the Mist," in *Volume IV* of this series, for more of these types of accounts).

According to her legend, Minnetunke seems to have been unlucky in love, or at least unlucky in her choice of whom to fall in love with. Rather than falling in love with a member of her own tribe or with someone from an allied tribe, she instead fell for a warrior from an enemy tribe across the river. Since they knew their love match would never be approved by either of their tribes, the lovers resorted to nocturnal trysts at a favorite precipice overlooking the river. But gradually, the two young people became less cautious about sneaking off to meet without being detected, and one night Minnetunke's suspicious father followed her to her secret meeting place. There he found the love-struck couple in a warm embrace, and taking one of the poisoned arrows he brought with him, he shot his daughter's sweetheart. As the wounded and dying man fell off the cliff, the broken-hearted Minnetunke leaped after him and was dashed to pieces on the rocks below. Ever after, says the legend, Lapachpeton is doomed to gaze forever from that same cliff, looking down on the rocks where his daughter met her death.[2]

Unlike Lapachpeton, Oneida chieftain Shikellamy holds a secure place in the annals of Pennsylvania's Indian history. However, his rock profile, like that of Lapachpeton's, may have succumbed to the elements. Either that, or it's very hard to see the profile today. But the fact that Shikellamy's stone profile may have fallen away or deteriorated to the point where it's no longer recognizable has not caused locals to remove their advertising sign. Along the river, opposite the high bluff called Blue Hill and by the Northumberland County town of Sunbury, there is still a sign with the words "See Shikellamy's Face." A small lookout area is reserved for those who want to stop and gaze at the visage, said to roughly resemble that of an Indian, that supposedly juts out from the side of Blue Hill across the river. But those who are attracted to the spot are in for a disappointment. No such visage is readily apparent anymore, and so one more natural memorial to Pennsylvania's Indians has apparently disappeared, swept away by the inexorable forces of nature that sooner or later remove all vulnerable traces of the past.

There was once also a quaint legend about the old Oneida chief that would have been carried away by the currents of time as well, had it not been preserved in the oral history of the region. The story comes down in part from none other than Conrad Weiser, illustrious Indian agent for the Penn family, and keeper of daily journals which held extensive accounts of his dealings with the Indians. Weiser and Shikellamy became close friends over the years, and between the two of them they changed the course of Pennsylvania's Colonial history. Both men died highly respected by Indian and frontiersmen alike, as evidenced by the fact that monuments were erected to honor the memory of both: Weiser's in the "Conrad Weiser Memorial Park" near Womelsdorf, Berks County, and Shikellamy's at his gravesite across from Blue Hill. Just how friendly Conrad Weiser and the Indians he dealt with were, can be deduced from the name they bestowed

---

2. Sarah A. McCool, "Schuylkill County Historical Gleanings," *Shenandoah Herald*, Schuylkill County, 1874.

upon him, which was *Tarachiawagon*, or Holder of the Heavens, but the friendship is also indicated by the aforementioned legend.

Dreams were thought by the Indians of that time to hold the key to the overall health of mind and body. They believed, in a surprisingly modern way, that one was interdependent on the other, and that wishes revealed in their dreams should be fulfilled in order to maintain a healthy state. Jesuit missionary Jerome Lalemant, writing in 1647, noted that Indians "throughout the countries of America of which we have knowledge, know not what it is to refuse what another has dreamed."[3] Another Jesuit, writing in 1656, also referred to the importance Indians placed in fulfilling another's dream wishes, noting "It would be cruelty, nay, murder, not to give a man the subject of his dream; for such a refusal might cause his death."[4]

Conrad Weiser, with his extensive knowledge of Indian customs and culture, must have been acquainted with the great respect the Indians held for one another's dreams. However, if he had forgotten about the custom, he was reminded of it one day in 1754. His friend Shikellamy had, the day before, expressed great admiration for a fine rifle Weiser was carrying. Apparently, the thought of the gun became a fixation in the old chief's mind. In fact, according to the legend, upon seeing Weiser the next day, Shikellamy told his friend that he had dreamed the previous night that Weiser gave him the rifle as a gift. Weiser knew he had no choice and was compelled to turn the gun over to the chief.

Realizing that it could work both ways, Weiser, several days later, told Shikellamy that he, too, had dreamed. His dream, said Weiser, was of Shikellamy giving him the beautiful Isle of Que in the Susquehanna. The legend states that Shikellamy gave Weiser the island, but as he did so was said to have stated, "Tarachiawagon, let us never dream again!"[5]

Although the story of Weiser's dream contest with Chief Shikellamy sounds plausible enough, similar versions of the story have been collected in New York, South Carolina, and Georgia. The names and places are always localized to the area where the story is found, but the basic story outline is kept the same. There is the Indian dreaming about a gun or knife, or other such coveted thing, and the frontiersman later dreaming of a nice

3. Paul A. W. Wallace, *Indians in Pennsylvania*, 92–93.
4. Ibid.
5. Ibid.

piece of Indian real estate. And the tale always ends with the Indian telling the other that they should dream no more. In New York State, for example, Chief Hendrick of the Mohawk tribe dreams of Sir William Johnson's scarlet uniform. Johnson, in turn, dreams of a large parcel of land, which causes the chief to lament that Johnson "dreams too strong" for him.[6]

The fact that variations of the dream contest story have appeared in several different places is an indication that the tale is merely a legend. On the other hand, perhaps one of the variations is based on fact and the others have arisen from it. While it is true that Weiser, and several generations of his descendants, once owned the Isle of Que (now part of present-day Selinsgrove), it is doubtful if he acquired it in a dream contest. We shall probably never have the satisfaction of knowing for sure what the truth may be, but there is no doubt that Conrad Weiser did experience the custom firsthand, and in his position as Indian agent, felt obligated to honor the belief. In one of his well-kept journals, the conscientious Weiser noted: "PS to buy a pipe with a Civern [case or covering?—JRF] over it and the best I can. To answer Saghsidowas dream."[7]

There are two other another interesting tales related to Shikellamy. Neither deals with him directly, but rather with his son, and one of the accounts talks of an entirely different kind of Indian face, that of the supernatural variety.

Although his Indian name was Tah-gah-jute, a title said to have been based upon his heavy dark eyelashes, his father Shikellamy later, due to the high regard he held for the man, gave his son the English name James Logan, after the man of the same name who was Secretary of Pennsylvania's Provincial Council. Tah-gah-jute's services to the colony of Pennsylvania during the French and Indian War were considerable, and he, too, became a close friend of Conrad Weiser.

Sometime after the war, probably in the summer of 1765, Logan left the Indian town of Shamokin where he had grown to manhood; and settled near present-day Reedsville in Mifflin County's Juniata Valley. Here he found a wonderfully pure and crystal-clear limestone spring on Kishacoquillas Creek, and by it he built his cabin. The spring is there to this day, and it is still known as Logan's Spring. (Kishacoquillas Creek was, by the

---

6. Ernest W. Baughman, *Type and Motif-Index of the Folktales of England and North America*, 340.
7. Wallace, Ibid, 93.

The historical marker at Logan's Spring. Located near Reedsville, Mifflin County, it commemorates the site where the cabin of this famous son of Chief Shikellamy's once stood.

way, named from yet another local Indian, a Shawnee chief of that name whose town, Ohesson, was located along the Juniata River on the site of present-day Lewistown.)

A number of Juniata Valley legends and accounts about the good Indian Logan arose over time, and all of them tell of how honest and decent he was, with one man who knew the old chief personally describing him as "the best specimen of humanity I ever met with, either white or red."[8] However, of all the local tales about Chief Logan, the one that captured the hearts of many people of that day and age was the story of the deerskin moccasins.

The account of Logan and the moccasins was claimed as a family heirloom by at least two families. The Browns based their claim on the fact that their version of the account came down from a daughter of William Brown, said to be the first settler in the Kishacoquillas Valley. It was his grandchild, so they said, that was the little girl mentioned in the legend.[9] But the Alexanders, on the other hand, say the little child in the tale was not a girl, but was the son of their ancestor James Alexander. It is perhaps

8. Sherman Day, *Historical Collections of the State of Pennsylvania*, 466.
9. Ibid, 468.

Logan's Spring. This ever-flowing stream was the water source for Chief Logan when he made this place his home near present-day Reedsville, Mifflin County.

the Alexanders who have the better claim, since James Alexander, in 1755, brought his family into the valley and settled at the spring which forms the source of Spring Run.

The site of the Alexander homestead was not more than a mile or two from their neighbor's spring and homestead. That neighbor was Chief Logan, and he and the Alexander family lived on friendly terms the whole time they lived close to one another. It took a while before Mrs. Alexander learned to trust her Indian neighbor, and her grief must have been almost unbearable one day, only a few weeks after they had moved there, when Logan carried off her son. The little lad had accepted and learned to trust Logan before the rest of the family, so when the chief suggested that he and the little tyke go back to his cabin so he could make him a nice pair of deerskin moccasins, the wide-eyed youngster readily accepted the invitation. Mrs. Alexander dared not resist. Her husband was away, and she was not capable of physically overpowering the strong Indian, so she resolved to endure the separation, hoping for the best.

Hours of "terrible anxiety" passed, until Mrs. Alexander decided she could stand it no longer and would rescue her son, no matter how hazardous the undertaking. So, the brave pioneer woman started out for Logan's cabin, probably with a musket on her shoulder. She had not gone too far before she saw Logan, with her son in his arms, coming toward her on the trail ahead. The elation and relief she must have felt when she saw that welcome sight can only be imagined, but she must have also felt some pangs of guilt when she saw the beautiful, beaded moccasins that Logan had just made for his little frontiersman.[10]

Perhaps the Browns and the Alexanders both have a legitimate claim to the legend after all. Given Chief Logan's sterling qualities and character, it would not be difficult to believe that this kind-hearted soul had bestowed the gift of new moccasins on more than one settler's child during the time he resided at his famous spring. On the other hand, it is difficult to understand why fate dealt Logan such a cruel hand after he left the beautiful valley of the Juniata.

Logan and his extended family migrated to the mouth of Yellow Creek, Ohio, in 1770; and it was here, four years later, that Daniel Greathouse and his band of frontier ruffians ruthlessly murdered many of Logan's tribe, including his mother, sister, and brother. It is said that it was this slaughter that caused the peaceful Logan to pick up the hatchet and scalping knife and seek revenge. His rampage lasted for six months and during that time the enraged warrior took thirty scalps before he finally declared that his thirst for revenge was now satisfied and that he would now "sit still" and not "lead or accompany any more war parties."[11]

10. J. H. Beers and Company, *Commemorative Biographical Record of Central Pennsylvania*, 444.
11. C. Hale Sipe, *The Indian Chiefs of Pennsylvania*, 440–444.

The loss of his family was not a wound that the scalps of Logan's victims could easily assuage. It was a burden he carried to his grave, and one he so eloquently described in what has been preserved in oratorical circles as the classic elocution known as "Logan's Lament."

"I appeal to any white man to say," so begins the famous lament, "if ever he entered Logan's cabin hungry, and he gave him not meat; if ever he came cold and naked, and he clothed him not. During the course of the last long and bloody war, Logan remained idle in his cabin, an advocate for peace. Such was my love for the whites, that my countrymen pointed as they passed, and said, 'Logan is the friend of white men.' I had even thought to have lived with you, but for the injuries of one man.

"He, this last spring, in cold blood, and unprovoked, murdered all the relations of Logan, not even sparing my women and children. There runs not a drop of my blood in the veins of any living creature. This called on me for revenge. I have sought it; I have killed many. I have fully glutted my vengeance: for my country I rejoice at the beams of peace. But do not harbor a thought that mine is the joy of fear. Logan never felt fear. He will not turn on his heel to save his life. Who is there to mourn for Logan?—not one."[12]

Whether Logan's spirit is satisfied and can rest in peace, after Logan died under violent circumstances in 1780, is for some an open question. Although nature seems to have thought it prudent to create a rock profile for his father, she apparently never felt impelled to create one for Logan. The Ohio Archeological and Historical Society, on the other hand, did erect a monument, bearing an appropriate inscription, near the historic elm tree where it is thought Logan delivered his famous lament. The monument as well as the famous speech, which has been translated into German, French, and other languages, insures that Logan's memory will live on, and will also insure that the world will always mourn the loss of one who, under the right circumstances, could have led mankind down a more peaceful and benevolent path.

Maybe it is that realization that will finally quiet Logan's spirit, if it has not been able to find peace over the last two-hundred and fifty years. There are those who believe that that rest has not come easily, if at all. Local farmers whose farms lie along Honey Creek and Kishacoquillas Creek have

12. Ibid.

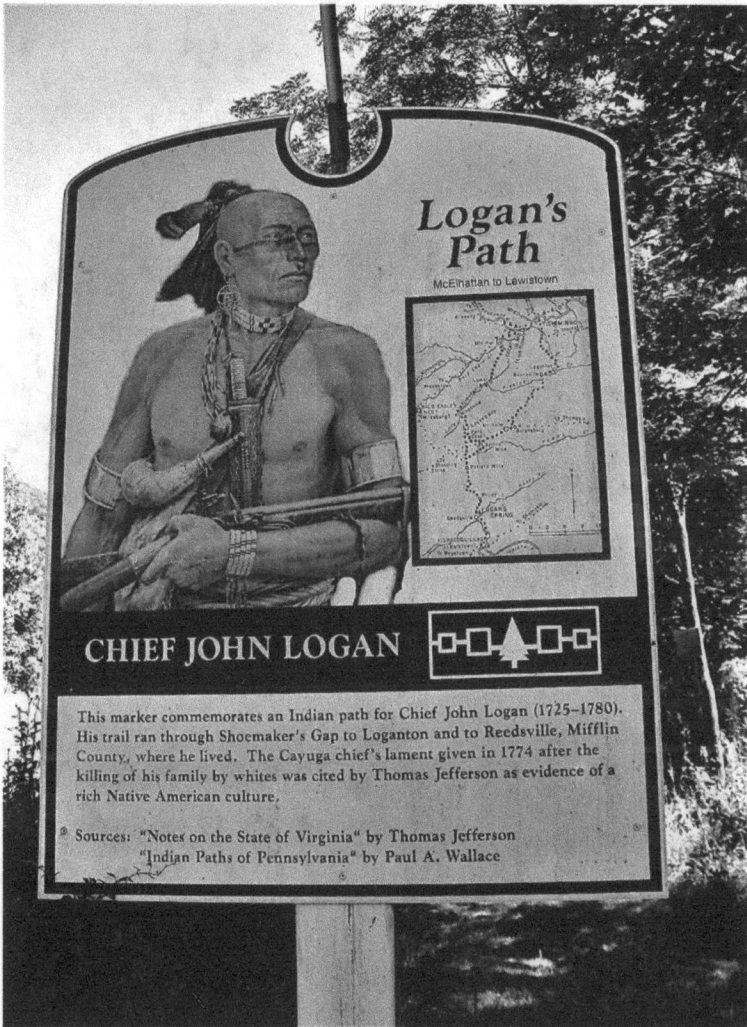

Logan's Path from McElhatten to Lewistown. Sign erected at the road leading to Shoemaker Park near McElhatten, Clinton County. It commemorates Chief John Logan's Path that went from here through Shoemaker Gap to Loganton and then on to his cabin site near Reedsville.

reported, over the years, of hearing the sounds of galloping horses running down through their fields and through the creeks. Usually, the sounds occur later in the day or at night, and whenever anyone tries to find the source of the mysterious hoof beats, they are unable to do so.

Some locals say that the horses, and their riders, are ghosts—spirits of the air with links to the area's Indian heritage. One farmer, who seems more

Memorial to Pennsylvania's native sons. This statue of chief Shikellamy stands at the Conrad Weiser Homestead historical site in Berks County. As Indian agent for the Penn family, Weiser was admired by the Indians because he treated them fairly and with utmost respect.

attuned to such things, claims he has, on several occasions, seen, on a knoll just outside his barnyard, the apparition of a lone Indian atop his horse. The ghostly riders, it is widely believed, are Chief Logan and his band of warriors, "running up and down the valley to see what's going on and to check everything out."[13]

13. Randy Dean (born 1963), recorded June 4, 1999.

The reason for Logan's perpetual vigilance, so say locals, is that "he was so upset about going to Ohio and leaving the area, and everything he left behind, that when he died, he came back."[14]

But there is another local theory that attempts to explain Logan's ghostly visitations, and that one states that Logan helped lead the bands of Indians who burned down Fort Granville, near present-day Lewistown, Mifflin County. The belief here is that it is the restless and dissatisfied spirits of these Indians that haunt the valley where they once lived and from which they sallied forth to burn the fort, during harvest time in 1756. Historians, however, would disagree.

Logan, historians note, did not move into the Juniata Valley until 1765, almost ten years after the fall of Fort Granville. Also, they note he did not "take up the hatchet" until provoked to do so by the murder of his family in 1774. It is recorded that followers of Chief Kishacoquillas, who lived just a few miles from the fort, warned nearby settlers of the impending raid, "enabling them and their families to escape to Carlisle."[15] It would therefore be easy to believe that if he had known about it, Logan, given his fondness for his settler neighbors at that time, might have issued warnings about the Fort Granville raid as well, rather than be involved in an attack that resulted in the fiery end to so many innocent lives.

But there is yet one other explanation that is offered by those who believe in the supernatural origins of the vapory forms that seem to haunt the valleys where Chief Logan and Chief Kishacoquillas once roamed. When construction of the new Route 322 Bypass reached the town of Reedsville, the project was halted for a while when workers uncovered what appeared to be an Indian burial ground. Fragments of Indian pottery and a number of human bones were inadvertently excavated, and the area was immediately cordoned off until archeological studies could be completed. Apparently, no one could prove that the area had been an Indian graveyard; or if such a conclusion was reached it was ignored, because the highway was not rerouted to avoid the site. Some now suggest that there were Indians buried here, and, with the Indians' strong belief that disturbing the final resting places of their ancestors causes restless ghosts, it is the ghosts of these ancient ones that flit along the picturesque creeks and hills of the Juniata Valley.

---

14. Ibid.
15. C. Hale Sipe, *The Indian Wars of Pennsylvania*, 296.

Memorial to Conrad Weiser. Also located at the Conrad Weiser Homestead historical site in Berks County, it preserves the memory of the man who served the early Commonwealth so well as Indian agent for the Penn family. Its symbols are not accurate since Pennsylvania Indians did not live in wigwams, and the musket shown is of Civil War vintage, not that of the French and Indian War.

NOTE: Since the first edition of this volume was published, some further details about the Isle of Que have surfaced that may shed some light on whether or not the Shikellamy/Conrad Weiser dream contest was a real event or not. Although it's true that Conrad Weiser did end up owning the Isle of Que, it's also a fact that numerous Indian skeletons were once unearthed on the southern end of the island, and that this site was known as a general Indian burying ground. Perhaps as a confirmation of that fact we can refer to an entry in Weiser's carefully kept journal, dated July 29, 1745. Here he states that the Mohawks, in telling him about a great alarm amongst them, mentioned that "the dead cry was heard everywhere, Que, Que, Que."[16]

It does not take much of a step in logic to assume that since the Isle of Que was in fact a true "Isle of the Dead," its name may have been derived from that fact. If so, then, given the Indian belief that the dead should not be disturbed, it seems highly unlikely that Shikellamy would agree to hand the Isle of Que over to Conrad Weiser in so flippant a way.

---

16. Jane Kessler, "Was the Isle of Que really Isle of Dead?" *Daily Item*, Sunbury, PA, November 23, 2009.

CHAPTER 10

MAKING THE MOON SHINE

Whiskey seems to have been a source of continuing controversy for Pennsylvania in its earliest days. The strong drink was a problem for the fledgling Colonial government when the first Indian traders began trading the "fire water" to the natives here, despite requests not to do so from both the government and some Indian chiefs, because of the inability of the warriors to handle their liquor in civilized ways. Just how inflammatory the issue could be was brought to the attention of Captain John Brady during the first years of the Revolutionary War.

Arriving at Frederick Derr's trading post near Fort Augusta, [present day Sunbury, Northumberland County] in 1776, Brady discovered some Indians drinking too freely from a barrel of Derr's rum. Knowing that the Indians had been in a warlike mood even before they started drinking, Brady overturned the barrel. Upon seeing the rum spill out onto the ground, one of the drunker Indians told Brady that one day he "would punish him" for what he had done. Brady knew the threat was not an idle one, and so maintained his guard until the Indians finally left the next day.[1]

Decades later the popular drink was still causing problems, culminating in the so-called Whiskey Rebellion, which occurred in southwestern Pennsylvania, in 1794, to protest an excise tax that had been levied on the liquid commodity. Here, in the counties of Fayette, Allegheny, Westmoreland, and Washington, the Scotch-Irish frontiersmen were both fond of their whiskey and united in their hatred of excise men. But their main concern was their loss of income.

---

1. John F. Meginness, *Otzinachson*, 478.

Rye, their principal crop, could only be transported by pack trains across the Allegheny ridges to markets in the east, and it was far more profitable to transport that rye in liquid form. Then, too, their product was a marketing success. Old Monongahela whiskey was famous, and it afforded them a handsome income.

At first the protests were mild, but they turned uglier when several tax collectors were tarred and feathered by angry distillers. Then things escalated to the point where stills of those who complied with the law were smashed by "Tom the Tinker" men, the name bestowed upon the more violent branch of the protestors.[2] At that point the Federal Government got serious about the matter. With the aid of fifteen thousand militiamen, led by President Washington himself, the rebels were brought into submission and the law was enforced.

Alcoholic beverages of all types besides whiskey, including brandy, hard cider, and beer, continued to be regarded by many as profitable commodities, even after taxes were levied and up until the Prohibition Era, when the Federal Government tried to turn every American into a teetotaler. The problem was that there were still, at that time, a lot of home breweries, a legacy from America's infancy. For example, it is said that in Centre County's Brush Valley there were, when it was just starting to be settled, "nine stills in operation before a single church was built." No strangers to the advantages of commerce, the savvy Brush Valley farmers shipped their liquor to Lewisburg on Conestoga wagons. From there it went on to Philadelphia, where it was exchanged for scarce goods like white sugar.[3]

The country populace as well as that in the cities both enjoyed their moonshine, a term they bestowed upon home-brewed whiskey no matter where it was made. But sometimes those who supplied the moonshine, and other brews like it, enjoyed drinking their beverages as much as their customers. It is recalled that the owner of Schwarzenbach Brewery in Germania, Potter County, wasn't ashamed of that fact.

Mr. Schwarzenbach had set up shop before Prohibition was enacted in 1920, and so, in an edict that flew in the face of those who opposed all drinking, he was allowed to remain open; people could still buy his beer

2. Edwin Valentine Mitchell, *It's an Old Pennsylvania Custom*, 117.
3. Mrs. Mary Abbot, interviewed April 17, 1976.

Sampling their wares. You had to make sure your moonshine was acceptable to sell to customers, or at least that's an excuse as good as any for getting drunk on your own distilled spirits - photo taken somewhere in the Pocono Mountains of Monroe County.

during those years when the national Prohibition Party was attempting to force total abstinence on the nation's populace.

Schwarzenbach's brewery sold small wooden kegs of beer called "Georgies," which were particularly popular, and an anecdote about how well Mr. Schwarzenbach liked his own brew was once a well-known story that made its rounds in Germania and the surrounding mountains of Pennsylvania's Black Forest. It seems that Schwarzenbach, despite his legal status, was hauled into court one day for some infraction he had committed during the course of running his brewery.

For some unknown reason, the judge in Coudersport asked Schwarzenbach if his beer was intoxicating. When the brew master replied that he didn't know, the judge then asked him how many glasses of his beer he drank in a day. "Oh, about thirty-five," came the surprising reply.[4] The story doesn't say what the judge's verdict might have been after that particular testimony, but maybe he was so amused that he dropped the charges. If so, it wouldn't have been the first time that it happened.

Up in the same section of Pennsylvania there was, about the same time, another brew master whose product was popular too. Moses Kenny's

---

4. Richard Braun, interviewed August 27, 1974.

White Mule whiskey was known far and wide as the best illegal booze in the Northern Tier. However, Moses' reputation eventually reached that of the authorities, and he was arrested and taken to Philadelphia to stand trial. There a judge with a sense of humor asked the defendant if he was the "Moses who can make the sun dark." Replied Moses, perhaps appreciating the judge's little joke, "Nope yer honor, but I'm the Moses that can make the moon shine!" Moses' descendants say that the judge was so amused that he let the old moonshiner go.[5]

Down in Clinton County there was yet another moonshiner whose reputation was even more widespread than that of Moses Kenny's, and Prince David Farrington had his share of troubles with the law too. The Prince, as he was known to locals, once had a run-in with Al Capone, who was unhappy with the business his illegal operations were losing to that of Farrington's, but Farrington handled the confrontation with Capone's thugs in typical fashion. He told them to tell Capone to "go to hell."

That seems like a foolhardy and unusual thing to do when a man from a remote spot like Sugar Valley is given a warning by a dangerous criminal like Capone, but Farrington was not your usual man. The first thing that marked him as unusual was his first name. Prince was his real first name, a tribute to a doctor in his hometown of Greensboro, North Carolina. The second thing that marked him as different was his lack of fear when dealing with danger and risk. Farrington was not face-to-face with the notorious Capone when he told him where to go, but the fact that he said it at all was enough to further enhance his own reputation as one of the most famous moonshiners in the state.[6]

Prince Farrington's bootleg booze operation was apparently big enough that it was a thorn in the side of Capone's own Chicago liquor business during Prohibition days, but Capone must have decided he could live with the problem after he heard Farrington's response. At least Farrington continued to do business as usual, right up until Prohibition was repealed in 1933. Prince continued making his whiskey after that, but the government was less tolerant since they were now getting tax dollars from every bottle of legal brew that was sold, and they didn't want anyone robbing them of their taxes.

5. James Y. Glimm, *Flatlanders and Ridgerunners*, 15.

6. Douglas C. Parker, "The Prince Who Died a Pauper," *Town and Gown Magazine*, State College, PA, November 1979.

Finally, the old bootlegger from Sugar Valley was convicted of tax evasion and spent two years in the Federal penitentiary in Lewisburg. From then on it was downhill for the Prince. He continued to run some stills until one night he was caught red-handed at one of his operations on Tangascootack Creek. Convicted once more, he fled to his home state of Florida, where five years later, he was caught and imprisoned. Paroled in a short time because of poor health, the old moonshiner lasted only another five years. He died in 1956 near Loganton, Pennsylvania.

Perhaps his first name helped mold him into the type of person he was, or maybe his first name was just a happy coincidence, but whatever the case may be, the people who knew Prince Farrington thought of him as a prince among men. It was because of this admiration that those who knew him liked to refer to him as "the Prince." Farrington was like a regal prince to those who worked for him and who dealt with him, because they knew that the owner of the Florida Fruit Farm, the name Farrington decided upon for his large plantation in Clinton County to honor his southern roots, was always willing to extend financial help to whoever needed it most.

Almost generous to a fault, Farrington doled out his ill-gotten gains in regal fashion. The farmers who grew the grain he needed for making his whiskey liked him because he paid them double for what they could have gotten for their crop on the open market. His neighbors around Williamsport and Lock Haven thought of him as a Robin Hood because he helped them pay their medical bills, buy their kids Christmas gifts, and saw to it that they got to the dentist so that their teeth were taken care of. Even law enforcement officials, many of them recipients of his largess too, liked the man they dubbed "the king of bootleggers." But that didn't mean that Farrington didn't have to watch his step.

Not every law enforcement official would look the other way when they discovered the Prince's operations, and sometimes that hurt economically. One bust that must have really been fiscally devastating for Farrington occurred the time the Feds stumbled across his still at Antes Fort, Lycoming County.

This was one of the Prince's largest operations, and the government men walked away with a quarter of a million dollars' worth of copper fittings. They also confiscated many barrels of whiskey for use as court evidence, but somehow the barrels walked off before the trial, and on that particular occasion they had to let Farrington off for lack of evidence (or, it might be said, they lacked the spirit to proceed).

No doubt it was episodes like the Antes Fort fiasco that forced Farrington to develop creative schemes to foil Federal agents, often referred to as revenuers by those who disliked them as much as the Scotch-Irishmen of western Pennsylvania hated the excise men of 1794. Deciding it would be better to use numerous hiding places for his barrels of liquor, the determined entrepreneur concealed them in farmers' haylofts or buried them in their fields, but it was the vast amount of sugar needed in the fermentation process that was hardest to conceal.

Boxcars, sometimes five or six at a time, would roll into town, and each car would be loaded with hundred-pound sacks of sugar. Railroad workers didn't ask what all that sugar was for, although most of them probably knew. The just unloaded them onto the railroad siding, and the next morning when they came to work the sacks would all be gone, just as though they had gotten up on their own and walked into the mountains.

That was the way it seemed to be, but everyone who was on the Prince's payroll knew how to keep their mouths shut, and one of Farrington's former employees was still somewhat reluctant to talk about his job when I interviewed him over fifty years after he had worked for the "King of bootleggers."

Eventually the old man loosened up and recounted the days he worked for "The Prince" in the 1930s. Born in 1921, he was about fourteen when Farrington hired him, but he remembered when, as a younger lad, he sat on Farrington's knee.

"Well, he wasn't a big man," said the former mule driver for the Prince. "He was kind of stocky, and he had a southern drawl to him. He was also kind of gentle and nice, and he was the savior of a lot of them farmers over there in Sugar and Nippenose Valleys when times were hard. He was their savior, you gotta remember that!

"You know at that time, too, the Prohibition people didn't want anybody to have whiskey around. That was moonshine days, and every day there was some revenue man around. They knew where it was coming from, and they was out to stick anybody they could. Well, I guess I was lucky because none of us ever got caught! We knew who the revenue men

Moonshining the way it used to be (Mount Pocono, Pennsylvania). Old-time photo of moonshiners somewhere in the "hollers" of Monroe County; they were not adverse to protecting the "goods" with their guns and unfriendly stares.

were, and just about where they was at! And Prince knew every one of them and where they stayed!

"His farm was between the towns of Rauchtown and Carroll, back on top of the mountain. He was quite a horticulturalist—quite a farmer, let's put it that way! He helped the farmers increase the production of rye and to develop better grades of wheat. But he also worked with cattle, and I attribute those damn mules more to him than to anybody else, but I can't say for sure.

"He was a southerner, and they had mules down there in the south. They trained their mules to work in the fields and cultivate cotton and corn. The slave followed them, but the mule was doing more than the slave did! So I assume Prince knew what he was doing, and I assume he was the one that trained these damned mules!"[7]

It was those "damned mules," rather than the Prince, that seemed to have left the most lasting impression on our storyteller. As part of his daily working duties when employed at the Florida Fruit Farm, the gentleman had used the mules to transport those bags of sugar that seemed to evaporate from local railway sidings after nightfall.

---

7. Howard Heggenstaller, recorded November 16, 1989.

The mule he seemed to get most often was a "whitish-gray" named Nellie, and it was this animal and others like it, that were used to transport barrels of whiskey and bags of sugar to and from the Florida Fruit Farm, which was known locally by the code name of "101 Ranch."

"You know, you didn't buy too much sugar at any one store, because it'd give it away," said the mule driver, recalling the purchases of sugar he and other employees would sometimes be asked to make locally. "Now you'd get a hundred, maybe fifty, pounds from this store, and fifty from that store, and gather it together to a farm. Or maybe a farmer would go to town and buy fifty pounds of sugar. You didn't buy it all at one time. Then when you got a load ready, why, it went to the still.

"You'd take the mule out and turn him loose. The mule went one way home and you went the other. Well, they'd take sugar back or grain back, and when he come out, he might have two ten-gallon kegs on him. And he went home.

"He went home himself. Hell, he knew what he was doing better than I did. He didn't know where he was going when he went back there, but after you turned him loose, he knew which way home was! He knew whether there was anybody on the road or anybody was watching. He did like any animal. They know better whether somebody is around than you do! He would go off into the mountains someplace, but eventually he'd come home. If he was going back with sugar and somebody was following him, that mule knew it. So did the other mules they used know it!"[8]

Although it's likely that stories of Prince Farrington's mules may no longer be heard today, the memory of the man no doubt lives on in Clinton and Lycoming Counties. The people in Sugar and Nippenose Valleys who still remember him, do so because they received kindnesses from him when they were children or because they are descended from someone else who did. No doubt they would all agree that the former mule driver's positive assessment of the man was accurate, but they might not feel quite the same affinity. "I have nothing against him," explained Farrington's former associate, "even if he was a bootlegger. So was my dad! "[9]

Those who drank Prince's moonshine, or that of any other bootlegger, might not have always looked back with the same fondness on these men

8. Ibid.
9. Ibid.

who "made the moon shine," particularly if they imbibed too freely and had an experience like that of one unfortunate drinker whose story was popular back in the same days that moonshine stills dotted the countryside.

The intoxicated man was walking home late one night after a round of heavy drinking at the local speakeasy, or so went the tale. Too drunk to walk straight, he soon wandered into the local graveyard. Here a newly dug grave lay waiting for its occupant, whose burial was to take place the next day. A moonless sky, combined with the alcoholic fumes clouding the man's brain, prevented him from seeing the deep hole in the ground that he was heading toward.

At first, he was totally confused after falling into the crater, but finally his besotted brain figured out what had happened. He immediately began to climb out of the pit, but the combination of the grave's steep slippery sides and the man's befuddled condition were more than a match for his frantic efforts to get out of his unpleasant predicament.

Rather than continue his unproductive struggles, the tired man gave up, and, overcome by the alcohol that was numbing his body, lay down in a drunken stupor. He had just settled into a nice sleep when he was rudely awakened by another man falling in on top of him.

A young beau, his thoughts on the girlfriend he had just visited, had decided to take a shortcut through the graveyard, and he too failed to see the booby trap. It was too dark, and he was too scared and confused, for him to notice that he had company in the pit. Just like the drunk had done, he, too, began to make desperate attempts to escape the dungeon in which he found himself.

However, the sides proved too steep and slippery to allow his escape also, but he valiantly kept trying while his silent and unseen companion looked on in mild amusement. Finally, the drunk couldn't stand to watch the young man struggle any longer, and, in a slurred voice of experience, wailed, "You'll never make it!" They say that the young beau made it out of that pit in one leap and never stopped running until he got home.[10]

---

10. Clarence Musser (born 1884), interviewed August 28, 1971 and November 12, 1971.

CHAPTER 11

TOUGH AS NAILS

Although Pennsylvania's big game animals were once found on almost every mountain throughout the Keystone State, the large mammals withered away like flowers killed by a heavy frost when the human species imposed its will upon the land. Bears, panthers, and wolves were no match for the settlers who indiscriminately slaughtered them, and deer and elk fared no better. Slowly the populations of all these animals decreased to a point where eventually every one of their species, including the deer, were almost nothing more than a memory in the minds of the men who once hunted them.

In this chapter are a few tales about the exploits of some of those old-time hunters, men whose lives and times can seem almost unbelievable to us today. However, these fragments of oral history, family traditions, and local legends foster mental images in our minds that lead us overpoweringly to the belief that hunting in those days was not for the faint-hearted. Hunters then had to be tough, as tough as nails might be one way of putting it, and the following episodes drive that point home.

Life on the frontier was always a hazardous proposition. Every day brought new threats to a frontier family's tenuous hold on their place in the wilderness, and when predators treated a farmer's livestock like it was their own private smorgasbord, it could not be tolerated. Frontiersmen used every means at their disposal to counteract the problem, and they succeeded with devastating effect. Poisons, firing of the forests to destroy habitats, grand hunts, ring hunts, and, finally, payment of bounties, were all used to protect the chickens, cows, pigs, and sheep that mountain families depended upon to survive.

However, this lethal combination of merciless hunting practices, even during the animals' breeding seasons, and destruction of their food sources and habitat, eventually wiped out some of the state's finest game species in the course of two hundred years. Moreover, it would appear that some of the greatest damage was done in the last twenty years of the nineteenth century, when lumbering operations reached their peak, and the repeating rifle appeared on the scene.

It was the money to be gained from the huge virgin forests of Pennsylvania that led the lumber companies to them. As a result, the animals that lived in those forests suffered two-fold. First their food supplies were destroyed along with the forests, and secondly, many of them were hunted down even more mercilessly as sources of food for the hungry lumber crews, or wood hicks, who were cutting down the trees.

Hungry lumbermen needed food, and lots of it, and one way to insure a steady supply was to hire professional hunters to bring it to them. It was these men, the "great white hunters" of the lumber era, who had made their living by collecting bounties offered by the state for the hides of panthers and wolves they killed, but who now could earn even more by providing deer, bear, and elk meat to the lumber camps. It is the exploits of these "market hunters," and others like them that form a unique chapter in the history of Pennsylvania, and it is their stories that follow.

Among the best-known professional hunters of their day were men like George Smith and William Long. Smith, who hunted the forests of Elk County, was credited with killing over 500 wolves, 3,000 deer, and an equal number of bear during his hunting career. Long, known as the "King Hunter" of Jefferson and Clearfield Counties, had a hunting record that was even more remarkable than Smith's. Said to be the slayer of 400 bear, 3500 deer, 50 panthers, and hundreds of foxes, wild-cats, and catamounts, Long also claimed the lives of 2,000 wolves.

Born in Berks County in 1794, the King Hunter claimed that he had gained his hunting prowess from the few expert Indian hunters that still roamed the forests of Potter County when he was a boy. From the time he was a young lad he had been an avid student of the hunter's art, and he claimed the Indians even taught him to howl like a wolf so he could call the animals up to within rifle range.

Perhaps it was this technique that allowed Long to amass the large number of wolf kills he was able to make over the years—a number apparently much larger than that of almost all his contemporaries. But whatever might be the case, it was the unrelenting toll taken by Long, and many other hunters of the same era, that finally put an end to that period I like to call Pennsylvania's "wolf days."

Even though his record of wolf kills was notable for the time in which he lived, Bill Long didn't have the last word on wolf hunting. There were others who employed hunting techniques that were just as devastating to the state's wolf population. One such man was Aaron Hall, whose grand brick mansion still stands along the Rattlesnake Pike on the mountain above Unionville in Centre County.

Hall's complete hunting record must have approached that of Bill Long's, but if it did not, then his record of wolf kills must have at least come close to that of the King Hunter's. According to Hall's granddaughter (born in 1915), the old hunter of the Alleghenies (born in 1830) would often keep a kerosene light burning in one of his mansion's back windows late into the night.

The light would attract some of the last packs of wolves that still roamed the wild woodlands on the high Allegheny Mountain tablelands to the north. Aiming and firing at one set after another of eyes that seemed to dart around randomly while emitting a greenish glow in the moonlight, Hall was able to down three or more wolves every night that he set out his luminous "bait."[1]

Of course, every country that made a determined effort to eradicate its wolf populations sooner or later had its last packs, its last wolf, and the killer of that last wolf. Over in England it is recorded that the dense and extensive forests of Blackburnshire and Bowland in Lancashire were "among the last retreats" of wolves in that area.[2] Here in Pennsylvania it was the Seven Mountains country of Central Pennsylvania and the Black Forest region of the Northern Tier that harbored some of the last wolves in the Keystone State.

---

1. Mrs. Ethyl Miller (born 1915), interviewed by telephone, September 7, 1987.
2. James E. Harting, *Extinct British Animals*, 155.

As to the slayers of those last wolves, the traditions in Scotland indicate that the last wolves in the wild and desolate stretch of moorland hills called the Findhorn were killed in 1743 by "MacQueen of Pall-a'-chrocain." Ireland, too, had its slayers of last wolves, and in County Tyrone that honor was handed to one Rory Carragh.

Both MacQueen and Carragh were fearless and determined hunters, and both were probably regarded as tough customers by their contemporaries. MacQueen, said to be the "most celebrated *carnach* of the Findhorn," was noted for his strength and height (a giant of a man, he stood six feet seven inches tall), and was reputed to have the best deerhounds in that part of the country.

Carragh's courage was also considered exceptional. Not a man could match it, as evidenced by the fact that when he decided to hunt down the last wolf pack in County Tyrone, he could not persuade any grown men to accompany him. He instead had to settle for the aid of a fearless young lad who served him well.[3]

Here in Pennsylvania there were, of course, men who rank with MacQueen of Pall-a'-chrocain and Rory Carragh as slayers of last wolves in the Keystone State. Records up in the Northern Tier of counties show that J. W. Starks was the last man to collect a wolf bounty in McKean County (1868), O. B. Fitch the last in Elk County (1877), Emanuel Dobson the last one in Forest County (1884), Levi Kissinger the final one in Tioga (1885)[4] with Laroy Lyman given the credit for one of the last taken in Potter County (1875).[5]

County histories and other historical records usually have little or nothing to say about these men who were the slayers of the last packs and the lone stragglers from those packs. Likewise, the historical record is often mute on the stirring events leading to the demise of Pennsylvania's wolf packs in general. There are a few exceptions to the rule, however.

Linn, in his *Annals of Buffalo Valley Pennsylvania*, for example, relates how a pack of frozen wolves was found on Shade Mountain, Snyder County, after the severe winter of 1834–1835. Apparently exhausted from hours of tramping through the heavy snows and weakened by the frigid weather,

---

3. Ibid, 177, 199–200.
4. William J. McKnight, *Pioneer Outline History of Northwestern Pennsylvania*, 178.
5. Samuel N. Rhoads, *Mammals of Pennsylvania and New Jersey*, 150.

Laroy Lyman (1821–1886); taken at age 44. (Photo courtesy of Krista Lyman, Roulette, Pa.)

they "appeared to huddle together," notes Linn, "eventually perishing from intense cold and hunger."[6]

In Blackman's *History of Susquehanna County* there are references to a great wolf hunt that took place in Franklin Township "on the waters of Snake Creek near the Salt Spring" shortly after Thanksgiving in 1818, and another in Silver Spring Township in 1834. Mentioned in the first case is the fact that 500 men participated in the drive that formed a circle of forty-seven miles. Blackman's passages provide proof of how serious the people of those times were about eliminating the wolf menace from their midst, but in the 1818 hunt their efforts went for naught. The final tally was "No wolves," notes Blackman, "and but one bear and one fox were captured."[7]

6. John Blair Linn, *Annals of Buffalo Valley, Pennsylvania 1755–1855*, 523.
7. Emily C. Blackman, *History of Susquehanna County, Pennsylvania*, 261, 468.

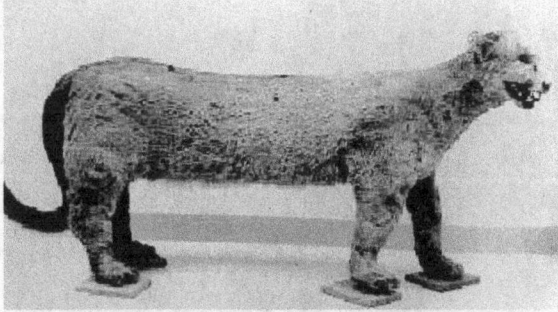

The Dorman Panther. A grainy photo of the panther shot by Lewis Dorman on Shriner Mountain of Centre County in 1857 (see the chapter titled "Phantoms of the Forest"). It was preserved for posterity by a skilled taxidermist. His masterpiece somehow ended up in the Ecology Lab at Albright College in Reading.

Blackman also gives the credit to one Joseph Fish for eliminating the last pack of wolves in Franklin Township of that same county. In the spring of 1830, a lone pack of the animals was harassing the settlers' livestock around present-day Lawsville, and Mr. Fish decided one day to pursue the marauders. He managed to capture seven wolf pups, but only later did he catch one of the old ones in a trap he had set in the same area. His efforts to rid the area of wolves were apparently effective, since after that time the settlers in the township had "little trouble" from that pack or any others.[8]

Settlers up around English Center and Oregon Hill, in Pine Township of Lycoming County, had a similar problem with one of the last packs of wolves in that section in the first half of the nineteenth century. The pack played havoc with settlers' livestock in that area for some time, taking particular delight in raiding the many flocks of sheep that were pastured on the hills.

It seemed to the settlers that the wolves were so bold that they would make an attack almost any time they desired. The arrogant predators would rush into the flocks, throttle the most docile animals, and then carry them over to their rocky dens along present-day Route 287 between English Center and Morris.

Local accounts here say that "old man English" and the Dowlings are credited with ending this nuisance by conducting repeated attacks on the

8. Ibid.

wolf dens. Any wolf that dared to make an appearance when the sharp-shooters were on the watch, paid for its insouciance with its life. The wolves are gone now, but the rocks where they made their infamous dens can still be seen today along Route 287.[9]

The killer of the last wolves in Centre County could easily have been Aaron Hall, but Jacob Auman might be a candidate for this distinction as well. At least one of Auman's descendants seemed to think so when he recalled the tale of how "one of the last wolves around" was caught by Auman in one of his traps. It was a story Auman's descendant had often heard as a lad from old-timers and from the elderly members of his family, and he was probably one of the last in the area to remember the details of this last wolf's demise in the section the early settlers here called the *Bind Schwamm*.

The Pine Swamp, with its dark hollows, marshy ground, rocky clefts, and steep ravines, was, and still is, an inaccessible place, but one well suited for a nocturnal animal like the wolf. In the earliest times, and right down to Jacob Auman's era, the virgin forest in the Bind Schwamm was so dense, and the trees so tall, that even at midday the sun hardly penetrated the thick forest mantle. The few sun rays that did breach the leafy canopy could only cast faint patterns of daylight on the spongy forest floor, and so it must have seemed like an ideal spot for the wolves, particularly in the fall.

It is then, during occasional autumn days when conditions are just right, that cool winds keep trees, dried grasses, and grey clouds in constant motion and cause shadows to dance and flit through foggy mountain gaps and across clearings in the woods. Such conditions would have made the wolves almost invisible if they decided to venture out of the daytime darkness of the Pine Swamp. As the animals darted down a hollow and up a mountainside, the swaying grasses, ferns, and hemlocks would have made their movements almost imperceptible, and the wolves would have been almost indistinguishable from the dark cloud shadows that moved along with them.

So, it was these conditions that led wolves, and the men who tried to trap them, into some of the wildest parts of the Seven Mountains country that lie due north of present-day Poe Valley State Park of Centre and Mifflin Counties. Here, between Second Mountain and Big Poe Mountain and

9. Howard Heggenstaller, recorded November 16, 1989.

in the small valley called Little Poe, can be found the Pine Swamp and the headwaters of Pine Swamp Run.

At these headwaters is an ever-flowing spring that bubbles up through red and white sands to become Pine Swamp Creek. The crystal-clear waters of this spring were a source of refreshment for the hunter and the hunted, and it was here that Jacob Auman placed the trap that caught one of the last, if not the last, wolves in the area.

"They had this trap on a stone that was laid in the water," recalled Jacob's great grandson. "There's good water there; the best. The wolf went there to get a drink, and he wanted to go across."[10]

For some reason the wolf threw caution to the wind. It apparently was not paying close enough attention to what it was doing, or perhaps it was not leery enough of the strange looking contraption sitting on the stone. Whatever the reason, the animal let its guard down, and its foot ended up caught in the metal clasp of the trap.

When Jacob Auman came by the next day to check his trap line, he was surprised to find the wolf. He shot and skinned the animal, but he didn't keep the hide. It would have been an interesting relic for his descendants to have today, but the hardy trapper was not interested in preserving family heirlooms.[11]

Wolves were not yet considered a thing of the past in those times, and their hides could still be redeemed for a bounty payment from the state. This hide, like those of all the other wolves the old man trapped over the years, went for bounty money, or for sale to others who perhaps had a better appreciation for keeping a memento of an age that was fading fast. Not only because the animals themselves were disappearing, but because the old-time hunters like Jacob Auman were fading fast as well.

Among the greatest of the old-time hunters of Pennsylvania's golden age of the hunt were Laroy Lyman and his father Burrel of Potter County. Burrel's father was one of the pioneer settlers in that county, coming there in 1810 and settling in a place later called Lymansville, in honor of his being the first settler there. Taught by his father to hunt and survive in the woods like an Indian, Burrel Lyman would later pass that same knowledge on to his son.

10. Quentin Confer, interviewed August 9, 1984.
11. Ibid.

Laroy's admiration for his father was boundless, and as a small boy he wanted to grow up to be just like him. Among Laroy's fondest memories were the times in winter when his father would come back from a long hunt, "his overshoes all snow and ice." The young lad would eagerly clean the icy hunting boots off, looking carefully for traces of blood to determine if his father had killed anything.

It seemed like an idyllic life to the young man, and in his later years, when he recalled those times and recorded them for posterity in his diary, he would remember that young man's thoughts and write "How I wished I was a hunter!"[12] And his wishes would come true.

Just like his father, Laroy Lyman would later become a wolf hunter, recalling in his diary that his father trapped wolves even before there were any traps in that part of the wilderness. The wolves were more prevalent and bolder in those days, and they had to be dealt with, one way or another. Laroy would also later recall that on those nights that he was late in getting home, the wolves would follow him, howling menacingly as they trailed behind.

Burrel Lyman was not one to sit back and take such threats mildly, and he counteracted the menace by designing his own wolf trap. Lyman's trap was nothing more than a wooden pen baited with a sheep, but it was ingeniously constructed so "wolves could jump in but could not get out."[13]

Born in 1821 in a log cabin in the Potter County wilderness, Laroy carried on the family hunting tradition as he got older. Numerous wolf packs still roamed the forests of old Potter County as Laroy grew into manhood, and in his diary, which is filled with pen pictures of those early hunting days, he recalls a night "up Fishing Creek" when a large pack howled and carried on so noisily around Weimer's sugar camp that a brush fence had to be set up around the camp "just to keep the wolves at bay."[14]

Remarkably by the time his hunting days in Pennsylvania were over, Laroy Lyman had killed over 300 of the fearful animals, bagging as many as seven in one day. Among those 300 were the members of one of the last packs in Potter County, a pack that preyed upon the livestock of the farmers who lived along Card Creek in Roulette Township during the winter of 1856, which was remembered as a very cold one with very deep snow.

---

12. Laroy Lyman, excerpts and information taken from a copy of his diary given to the author by Krista Lyman, Roulette, PA.

13. Ibid.

14. Ibid.

In a diary entry dated January 17, 1856, Laroy Lyman writes that wolves killed four of his neighbor's sheep the previous night. The following day's entry then notes that he and his neighbor, John K. Burt, "watched last night for wolves," seeing "one early in the evening and one about midnight." Then the diary entries indicate that another wolf was spotted at the barn the next night, and the next day Lyman and several others tracked it to Card Creek and shot it.

Lyman and several hunting companions then set up a watch at Reuben Card's barn that night and maintained their vigil for six more nights without spotting a single wolf. It was then decided that they would stand guard one more night, a night that frigid temperatures would prompt Lyman to later describe as "the coldest night I ever saw in my life; the mercury went down in the ball."[15] But the extra effort paid off and one more wolf was spotted and shot.

For the next week the remaining wolves in the pack were trapped and shot until there were only three left. Then on February third, Laroy harnessed his team of horses to his sleigh, bundled up his wife and daughter Sybil, and headed down the "dugroad east of Burtville." Determined to eliminate the last wolves no matter how much time and effort it took, Lyman planned to take his family to Reuben Card's and then go on a solitary hunt. However, the hunt that day turned out to be a short one.

The arctic winter temperatures had caused the waters of the Allegheny River to freeze solid, and as the sleigh bounced over the dugroad beside the river, the Lymans must have pulled their horsehair blankets more tightly around them to try to keep warm. Then suddenly Sybil Lyman spied movement on the ice.

"Oh, Pa," she exclaimed. "See that dog running on the river ice!"

The "dog" was a large wolf. Whipping his horses into a run, Lyman headed off the animal as it came out of a swamp. Jumping out of his sleigh, he drew a bead on the wolf with his rifle and laid it low with his ball. Upon close inspection it was found that the dead wolf was the three-legged one that had vandalized so many farmers' sheep for so long.

The general populace was anxious to hunt down the last two wolves, and a big hunt was commenced. One wolf was tracked over into the hills of McKean County, and then chased back to the head of Card's Hollow.

---

15. Ibid.

Here the hunters left him, but the next morning his tracks could be seen all around Card's barn, where the vicious killer had hoped to help himself to another sheep.

The hunters took up the chase once more, but it wasn't too long before they found the wolf in one of Laroy's traps that he had lent to Reuben Card. Lyman took it alive, later taking it around to schools to show to children who he knew had never seen a live wolf before, but when the exhibition tour was over, the showman killed the star of his show.

Then on February thirteenth, he got word that the last wolf had been caught in another of Card's traps, but that Card needed some help. When Lyman got to the Card farm, he found a crowd of onlookers milling about Card's barn. The wolf, he was told, had crawled under the barn, the trap still attached to its leg, and no one would volunteer to go in and get it. Seeing a rake nearby, Laroy took it, crawled under the barn, and caught the trap's chain in the rake's teeth. Slowly backing out from under the barn, he dragged the wolf after him. Once the animal was out, the onlookers made short work of it using guns and clubs.[16]

Few men today would be up to the task of crawling under a barn to pull out an angry wolf caught in a trap, but that was the point of this chapter; that is, to let the reader know that there once were hunters who could muster the courage to do such things; or, as some today would say, were foolhardy enough to do so. Regardless of how you think about it, it seems safe to say that men who hunt like Laroy Lyman and other rugged hunters of times past are few and far between today.

Perhaps the rigors of those days called for tougher men, or perhaps the abundance of animals like the panther and the wolf inspired men to be tough. Whatever the case may be, we can only look back today in wonder and disbelief. Times and men like these will probably never come again to the mountains of the Keystone State, and perhaps we all lack something because of that. These men and their stories come from a wild and romantic chapter of Pennsylvania's past that was unique. It was unique not only in terms of ecological conditions, but also in terms of lifestyle, morals, and ethics.

Although there were things in that culture we don't admire today, we seem so far away from the very best parts of it sometimes that we need to slow down, look back, and try to see what we've lost. If we don't, we'll end

16. Ibid.

E. N. Woodcock and his bear traps. This Potter County hunter and trapper (born in 1844) was as tough a customer as they come. Woodcock's many adventures in the Black Forest of Pennsylvania might rival those of more famous wilderness trailbalzers. His exploits can be found in his autobiorgaphy titled "Fifty Years a Hunter and Trapper."

up reducing life to a series of debits and credits, with no appreciation for the simpler things of life. Things like the whisper of the wind in a lonesome pine, the colors of the sunset at the "golden hour," a majestic view from atop a mountain, or the lure of the wild, which even yet today in the remoter parts of Pennsylvania may include the howl of the wolf or the cry of the panther. Perhaps if we slow down long enough to look and to listen, we'll find that the wild and romantic era of Pennsylvania's past is not so very far away after all.

CHAPTER 12

INDIAN PEG

Tales of Pennsylvania's Last Indian Maidens

Over the course of time, it seems that history has been kinder to Pennsylvania's Indian men than it has been to its Indian women. Probably every section of Pennsylvania has had its "last" Indians at one time or another, and anecdotes about some of them have been preserved in the historical record. In his *History of the Juniata Valley*, for example, the historian U. J. Jones claims that the last Indians residing in that part of Pennsylvania were men named Job Chilloway, Captain Logan, and Shaney (or Shawnee) John. Jones also includes some additional biographical information on each man, but he fails to mention anything about the last surviving members of the female branch of the Juniata Valley's Indian people.

In Dauphin County it is recorded that one of the last, if not the very last, Indians there was "Indian Joe." The legend about him and about an unusual rock formation overlooking Clarks Valley is included in the author's story titled "The Kings Stool," in *Volume I* of the *Pennsylvania Fireside Tales* series.

Similarly, the memory of Schuylkill County's last Indian has been preserved in a history of that area. Described in the derogatory terminology of that time as a "half-breed," Big Jack lived in a ramshackle hut that sat upon one of the hills overlooking Pottsville during the early decades of the nineteenth century.

Most of the time he kept to himself, but occasionally he would come to town to peddle woven baskets he had made and which he sold to support himself. However, the residents of Pottsville apparently heard the man more than they saw him, for it was Big Jack's custom at sundown to stand outside his cabin door and shout war whoops and other blood-curdling Indian calls.[1]

Even though other interesting accounts might be found concerning the last male members of Pennsylvania's Indian tribes, it is the intent of this essay to present some narratives about a few of the last female members of the state's aborigines—the Indian women whose memory lives on in both the oral and written history of the Keystone State. As noted earlier, the historical record has few such references, but the memory of one old Indian woman and her "sanitary" cornbread was preserved in the oral history of Perry County.

Older residents of that county in the first decades of the twentieth century often recalled that, when they were younger, they had heard elderly natives of western Perry County tell of an Indian village that once stood in the shadow of Bowers Mountain, near what is now the village of Cisna Run in Madison Township. For many decades after the region had been settled, an abandoned log cabin that predated them by an unknown number of years could be seen on a high knoll on the north side of Sherman's Creek, seemingly impervious to both the weather and to settlers' takeover of former Indian lands.

How long the old place had stood there, no one was sure, but its condition and construction indicated that the builders had been Indians, and so it was concluded by many that it was a lone survivor of the old Indian village. No proof of that fact can be unearthed today, but the idea is somewhat supported by the oral history of the Tuscarora Mountains, which indicates that the solitary log cabin was a lingering reminder of one of the last members of the Indian tribe that once called this place their home.

The story of the old building has come down to us today through descendants of the Cisna family, who came to the Blue Mountains with other Scotch-Irish settlers, sometime in the first half of the eighteenth century. The Cisnas were the first to settle where a small stream empties into present-day Sherman's Creek, and they were recognized for their frontier spirit when that little stream was named after them, with the village that grew up there eventually adopting the same name.

At that time there was an Indian woman living nearby in the small log hut that was erected by her tribesmen in the distant past. Being on

1. George Korson, *Black Rock, Mining Folklore of the Pennsylvania Dutch*, 152–153.

friendly terms with settlers, the native woman, whose name is no longer remembered anymore, decided to introduce herself to her new neighbors, and so came calling on Mrs. Cisna one day.

Mrs. Cisna graciously invited her caller into the Cisna cabin, and as a token of friendship asked her if she would like some cornbread. When her visitor replied that she would indeed be glad for such a treat, Mrs. Cisna got out the proper ingredients. However, before she put them all into a mixing bowl, she carefully washed her hands. Then, after drying off her hands, the hospitable hostess kneaded the cornmeal, milk, and other components, together into a nice yellow dough, and baked it. Once the bread was ready, the two neighbors sat down to a hot cup of tea and slabs of fresh-baked cornbread.

Mrs. Cisna, not too long afterwards, decided to pay a visit to her Indian neighbor, and in turn was invited into the Indian lady's modest dwelling. During the course of the conversation the daughter of the forest asked her guest if she'd like to have some of her cornbread, and Mrs. Cisna replied that she would.

Following Mrs. Cisna's example, and desiring not to offend, the Indian lady put water in a large bowl and made a quite a show of washing her hands. However, instead of dumping that water out of the wash bowl, she then proceeded to mix the ingredients for cornbread into that same water.

It is said that Mrs. Cisna, not wishing to offend her hostess, ate of this "sanitary production." It must have taken some willpower to do so, considering the unappetizing way in which the bread had been produced, but apparently Mrs. Cisna was not harmed by the baked goods. She lived, say the old tales, "to a ripe old age."[2]

The Perry County folktales don't indicate what eventually happened to the old Indian who lived at Cisna Run, nor do they reveal how she died or where she's buried. However, over in Chester County there once lived another Indian woman who fared somewhat better in that regard.

A memorial to her can still been seen near the junction of Routes 1 and 52 in that county, but it's probably become such an accustomed part of the everyday landscape that passersby today don't even give it a second look. However, if they were to stop and read it, they would find that it was erected in 1925, under the auspices of the Pennsylvania State Historical Commission and the Chester County Historical Society.

2. H. H. Hain, *History of Perry County, Pennsylvania*, 44.

The bronze tablet on the memorial stone notes that it was placed here to mark the birthplace of Indian Hannah, "the last of the Indians in Chester County," and that she was "of the Unami Group, their totem the tortoise, of the Lenni-Lenape or Delaware Indians."

Born in 1730 in a vale near where the marker sits today, Hannah lived to a comparatively old age for those days, dying in 1802 at age seventy-two. Today we would attribute her fine health and long life to good genes, but her fellow Indians would have had a different explanation.

They would have recalled that baby Hannah, like other Indian papooses of her era, was made hardy by being immersed in a pond, in the valley where she was born. The pond was not regarded by the Indians as having any special magical powers compared to other bodies of water, nor were its waters always warm like those of six unusual springs in Perry County.

Although it's a bit of a diversion from the story of Indian Hannah, I would be doing the reader a disservice not to provide some further details on one of Pennsylvania's most unusual natural wonders. Located along the Blue Mountains, near the village of Bridgeport in Perry County, there is a secluded forest glen that at first look appears to be swampland.

However, the unusual nature of this swamp only becomes evident in the wintertime when clouds of hot mist hover over the boggy terrain and the pools of water never freeze, even in the coldest weather. Geologists have confirmed that the temperature of the wetland's waters, which arise from six different springs, stays at a constant sixty-six degrees.

This is the little-known Warm Springs of Pennsylvania; probably the only one of its kind in the state, and perhaps one of very few in the east. Even as early as 1830 the springs were heralded for their curative powers, attracting stagecoach loads of visitors who came to bathe in the waters and drink them, hoping to cure such ailments as "rheumatism, kidney and liver complaints, dyspepsia, eczema, sore eyes, and general weakness of the constitution."[3]

The spring or pond into which Indian Hannah of Chester County was immersed when she was a mere papoose was certainly not a warm spring, nor did the Indians feel it had curative powers relative to other springs. It was merely the Delaware Indian custom in the wintertime to take their newly born children and immerse them in the icy waters of a nearby pond or lake, sometimes having to use their tomahawks to break through the thick ice that

<hr>

3. "Warm Springs Discovery Made," author unknown, *Perry County Times*, July 7, 1977.

had formed on the surface. This frigid baptism, they believed, would imbue the children with a hardiness that would guarantee a long and healthy life.

Not much else is known about Indian Hannah, other than the fact that in the wintertime she made brooms and baskets, and in the spring and summer she would wander from place to place selling them. She was often seen riding her horse, followed by a few pigs and her two dogs. However, it is said that she was afraid of thunderstorms, and when one arose, she would hurriedly leave the area until it had passed.

She was much loved by the predominately Quaker settlers of the area, and it was they who took turns keeping her in their homes when she could no longer support herself. It was the same kindly people who contributed the funds needed when it came time to place her in the Chester County Home as one of its first residents in 1800. It was here that she died, her last resting-place marked with another large boulder and bronze tablet.

It is said that Indian Hannah, despite her many years of mingling with her neighbors, maintained her Indian character and pride in her people until her dying day. Known for her "proud and haughty spirit," she avoided the baser class of settlers. But it was evident to her friends that she nursed a sorrow which she could neither mend nor shake off. To her dying day she was heartbroken over the treatment that her people had received, and she often spoke of those many "wrongs and misfortunes" as though trying to assuage her grief.[4]

On the other hand, Hannah would not have been alone in her malaise. There was another Indian woman who once lived in a different part of the state, who would have understood Indian Hannah's despondency if she had been told about it. And her understanding would have come from experiences that were diametrically opposed to those of Indian Hannah.

The story of one of the last Indian women of York and Cumberland Counties' South Mountains is not a particularly pleasant one, but it does provide an opportunity to refer to yet another water source in the Keystone State, and it perhaps also holds the explanation as to how that spring received its name. Even up to this day the story has links to families that may be offended by the narrative, and so the old gentleman who passed the tale on to me wasn't sure how to proceed.

"I've always been a little bit hesitant on how or what I say about this because I don't want to get in trouble with the K— family in Cumberland

---

4. C. Hale Sipe, *The Indian Chiefs of Pennsylvania*, 174.

County," began the man whose ancestors had befriended the Indian woman they knew as "Indian Peg."

"Over in Cumberland County we had ore banks, and they were originally operated by the K— family," continued our storyteller, as he related to us the tale that had been passed down through five generations of his family.

"Now on the other side of the mountain there's a place called Beavertown, in York County. Adam Baish and his new wife Mary, known as Molly Wonders, settled over there on a farm along the mountain back of Beavertown sometime in the early 1800s. It was part of the South Mountains on that ridge that rises up right from Dale's Gap. They were Quakers, and the church they attended is still in existence.

"Shortly after Molly started housekeeping there on the farm, her first child was born, and she needed help. Nobody was around, but an old Indian lady came along wanting something to eat, saying she would work for her keep and that her name was Indian Peg. So, Molly Baish would furnish her with food, and she would come over and help with the housework or anything else Molly needed.

"Indian Peg lived over on the Cumberland County side of the mountain. She had a hut there; I've seen the foundations up there in the gap; and she would walk into Carlisle to do her marketing. One night Molly Baish heard a wailing over the mountain. Now I can't picture sound carrying that distance, but Molly supposedly heard this wailing and weeping. By this time her children had grown up pretty good, and I understand her Johnny, the oldest, was about twelve when this happened.

"She gave Johnny a lantern and said, 'It sounds like something's wrong over with Peg. You go over.' So he went over and found that someone had destroyed her hut when she was away at market in Carlisle. He brought her back home with him, and the Baish's allegedly built her a cabin on their property. Peg lived there, died, and was buried at the cabin site.

"Well K— had wanted Molly Baish to get rid of Indian Peg. They didn't want any Indians around, and allegedly he's the one who destroyed Peg's hut while she was gone. He had insisted that the Baishes drive her out, and they had refused to do it. In fact, Molly Baish told him 'Someday you'll have retribution for this!'

"Well K— would work his ore banks along with his men, and he was a pretty heavy drinker. In fact, he used to bring his whiskey along with him when he come over, and to get it good and cold he'd put it in a spring over there. So, one day he was over there, and he was in pretty good spirits at the time. He got on his horse and started across the stream, but the horse threw him, and he went down into the stream and drowned—in less than eight inches of water!"[5]

After hearing his tale, we had to agree with our storyteller that the only memory of Indian Peg left today is the melancholy narrative of her mistreatment. However, on second thought, it also occurred to us that there is one other reminder of the old lady that remains, and that would be the name of the little spring that is indirectly linked to her story. On local maps, and to those who live around it, the small spring where K— chilled his bottles of whiskey is still referred to as Whisky Spring. Future generations will no doubt look at that name and wonder why it was chosen for this particular place, but readers of this book will not have that problem, for, in the words of radio commentator Paul Harvey, you now know "the rest of the story."

NOTE: There is yet another Indian maiden who should be mentioned in this chapter. A monument that preserves her memory, the last of her race in the West Branch Valley, could once be found along Nichols Run Road near Jersey Shore, Lycoming County. It may still be there, but even years ago it had become so weathered as to be almost unreadable. However, when I first saw it back then, I noted that embedded at the top of the monument was an engraved plaque which read as follows:

SHAWANA
Daughter of Old Nichols
A Friendly Seneca
The last Indian girl in the
West Branch Valley
Died February, 1853
Aged 16 Years
Erected by Fort Antes Chapter DAR
and Col. Henry W. Shoemaker
1918

---

5. Ralph Kinter (born 1915), recorded June 6, 1989.

CHAPTER 13

DARK CLOUDS AND
MISTY MOON

Oftentimes the picture of the olden-time Pennsylvania that leaps from the pages of the *Pennsylvania Fireside Tales* books is that of a land of romance where the daily grind was a much slower-paced and more carefree time than the life we lead today. It does seem true that people back then, in those times in which these fireside tales originated, were more often satisfied with the simpler pleasures of life; less dissatisfied with what they didn't have and more appreciative of the things they had.

On the other hand, human nature hasn't changed that much over the centuries, and folks today are still just as likely as their ancient ancestors to be troubled with the same doubts and fears. Among those fears are the ones that owe their origins to a belief in otherworldly things; seemingly supernatural events and entities that sometimes emerge unexpectedly to complicate mankind's view of the natural order.

There is no doubt that legends and folktales often contain a strong dose of that supernatural element, regaling us with accounts of phantasmagoric images, restless spirits, wicked witches, goblins, and other things that go bump in the night. Whether it's because we've heard such tales all our lives or because we've inherited a healthy fear of the unknown from preceding generations, it seems we all have a natural tendency to keep the supernatural at arm's length. Although some of us are more apt than others to be scared out of our wits over such things, the inclination to be afraid of them is there, and most probably will always be a part of human nature. It's that very same nature that's no doubt responsible for the abundance of so many tales of this type, both in the past and in their continuing appearance today.

There are few of us who wouldn't experience some forebodings about spending a night alone in a house that has a reputation and an appearance of a haunted place; an abandoned and shuttered homestead where no one has lived for years and no one today wants to live there because of its creaking floors, sagging roof, and strange noises, like groans or clanking chains, that seem to emanate from its least accessible parts when dark ribbons of clouds dim the hazy light of the harvest moon as they silently glide over its face.

Whether someone believes in them or not, supernatural topics do seem to appeal to everyone as an intriguing form of entertainment—either in the form of books, movies, or oral presentations. So, whatever your opinions about these types of anecdotes, the tales that follow are presented in this chapter for you to enjoy or to denigrate; whatever best fits your belief system.

They represent two of the most unusual "spook" stories I've encountered in over thirty years of collecting legends and folktales all over Pennsylvania, and they are not inventions from this writer's imagination, but are a part of Pennsylvania's legendary treasure house.

As such, they are preserved here in hopes that future generations might someday uncover this small part of my own legendary lode and derive some enjoyment from them. The first tale is that of a haunted cemetery in Lancaster County, while the second is about a strange and persistent image on a jail cell wall in Carbon County.

HANS GRAF'S CURSE

Belief in the possibility of werewolves, the idea that some men could transform themselves into wolves, is thought by some to have originated with the Greeks. Among the fascinating legends of the Greek Isles is the story of Lykaon, king of Arkadia, who invited the god Zeus to dinner. Lykaon, to test the god's omniscience, decided to serve him human flesh as the main course. Displeased with this impertinence, Zeus is said to have transformed the king into a wolf.

The Hans Graf Cemetery and wall. Located along the Old River Road between the Lancaster County towns of Bainbridge and Marietta, it has a chilling story.

Each year thereafter, according to the ancient accounts of Roman chronicler Pliny, a noble Arkadian was led to the edge of a lake. Hanging his clothes on the limb of a tree, the nobleman then plunged into the lake and was immediately transformed into a wolf. It was a curse that lasted for nine years and would only be lifted if the changeling had refrained from tasting human flesh during the nine-year period. If he had managed to abstain from that temptation, the nobleman was then allowed to swim back to where he had hung his clothes and put them back on, whereupon he returned to his natural form.[1]

Fantastic as such ideas may have sounded to more enlightened people who lived long after the decline of the Roman Empire and the disappearance of the ancient Greeks, belief in werewolves didn't disappear during the Middle Ages in Europe. It was a notion that was prevalent there during the 15th century, particularly in the Carpathian Mountains of Romania where legends of werewolves and of Transylvanian prince Vlad Tepes were widely circulated and believed. During those early times when last names had not yet become commonplace, Tepes, whose father's name was Dracul, was simply referred to as "son of Dracul," or in the Transylvanian style, "Dracula."

The prevalence of werewolf legends there, and the tales of Dracula's penchant for impaling his enemies on sharp wooden spikes and putting

1. John Fiske, *Myths and Myth-Makers*, 69, 70, 79–85, 89.

Another view of the Hans Graf Cemetery. Parts of the old burial ground are becoming choked with weeds and many of the old tombstones are hidden behind them, but the gravestone of Hans Graf is nowhere to be found.

them on public display, formed the inspiration for Bram Stoker's famous story of Count Dracula. And to this day, tourists flock to those same Carpathian Mountains to visit the real Dracula's castle and his granite tomb on the island monastery of Snagov.[2]

Over the last several centuries there have been a number of theories proposed to explain the origins of the belief in werewolves, many of them referring to peoples' inability to understand the physiological basis for shocking medical afflictions like porphyria, cataleptic fits, and hypertrichosis. Porphyria, caused by allergic reactions to both garlic and sunlight, can cause acute pain and leave its victims with prominent teeth and hairy faces, while the primary symptom of hypertrichosis, also known as werewolf syndrome, is a coat of thick hair over every square inch of the afflicted one's body.

Despite these scientific explanations, the belief in werewolves still appeals to gothic types who seem to relish the idea that such monsters once existed. As a result, it's those types who probably keep alive the legend of a werewolf that is said to protect a small family cemetery near one of the Susquehanna's river towns in Lancaster County.

Situated back of the small town of Rowena and along the Old River Road between the Lancaster County towns of Bainbridge and Marietta,

2. Lois Fagan, "Try This Trip with a Transylvanian Twist," *Sunday News*, Lancaster, PA, October 28, 1990.

the Hans Graf Cemetery is a forgotten place. No doubt regarded as just another old family plot; the burial ground probably elicits few passing glances from those who whiz by here in their automobiles. But there are those who, from time to time, do take a moment to stop and investigate the lonely vale.

No doubt many are drawn to it because they want to find out who lies here and when they lived. However, the thing that probably attracts most of those who pull over and get out of their cars is one particular tombstone among the thirty or more that stand like silent sentinels over the final resting places of the graveyard's inhabitants.

The cemetery is somewhat unique because it has no entrance gate. The only way into the graveyard is to step over a four-foot-high stone wall that surrounds the sacred ground. In the wall facing the roadway is a stone bearing the notation "Within this God's acre rest the descendants of Hans Graf."

It's an inscription that only adds to the mystery of the place, and as the visitor reads the markings on the tombstones here, most of which are in old German script with dates back to the late 1700s or early 1800s, they may even begin to feel that they are trespassing; that they have been transported back to another time and place and are disturbing those who inhabit that sphere. But according to the legend that clings to this spot, that's exactly how Hans Graf wants them to feel.

Forty or more years ago, the graveyard was a favorite hangout for local teenagers who wanted to scare their friends. Drawn there by its legend and

The sign on the wall at the Hans Graf Cemetery.

by the deserted Graf homestead standing nearby that at that time looked exactly like a haunted house out of a Hollywood horror movie, area teens seemed to enjoy the thrills the place afforded. It was not uncommon to see them there as the Halloween season approached, and especially upon the arrival of the Autumnal Equinox.

The legend that attracted the thrill seekers to this spot was that of Hans Graf's curse. Hans Graf, says the old tale, was a werewolf who placed a curse on the place where he and his descendants are buried, and it is his spirit that still protects the hallowed ground. According to locals who still remember the tale, Graf's curse is not all-inclusive because it does not affect casual visitors, only venting its wrath upon those who dare to walk around the top of the cemetery wall seven times in succession, and then only during the full moon of October.

Any living descendants of Hans Graf are no doubt mortified by the longevity of the old tale. Some local historians would share a like disdain for the legend, no doubt pointing out that some accounts indicate that his English neighbors thought so highly of Graf that they referred to him as The Earl, a title of an English nobleman, and used it when naming their East Earl Township in Lancaster County.

Then there are other locals who believe that the legend was nothing more than a story concocted by parents to keep their kids from vandalizing the cemetery and its wall. Similarly, there are still others who point out that there is something missing in the old cemetery that, by its absence, discounts the legend entirely.

Those stopping to take a closer look at the grave markers in the old Graf burial ground will be immediately struck by the fact that there is no tombstone marking the final resting place of Hans Graf himself. The old man's gravestone, with its epitaph in elaborate German script, could still be seen there, up until about fifty years ago. About then someone carried it away, perhaps as a morbid souvenir or as a prank to show their friends they were brave enough to defy the curse that supposedly protects the place. Others would say that the theft was a foolhardy act, because the culprit who took the stone may, if he hasn't already, someday succumb to the terrible consequences of the curse. And those who feel that way point to the fate of one teenager who, in the 1960s, defied the curse too.

When he reached adulthood, town constable Thomas Wohlfiel of Elizabethtown was still not a believer in curses or vampires, an attitude that hadn't changed from the time he was a teenager and had gone to the Graf cemetery one night with some friends. Wohlfiel knew about the cemetery's curse, and the claim that anyone who walked around the top of its wall seven times in the full moon's light would not survive to see the sun set the next day, but one night he decided to make that walk anyway.

The brave teen made six and one-half trips around the top of the graveyard's wall before his friends pulled him off. It appeared as though they had done him a favor, for the young man grew into adulthood and seemed to have escaped the punishment of the Graf curse. Thomas Wohlfiel became a successful part of the constabulary in the Elizabethtown area, responsible for protecting the property and rights of law-abiding citizens, and even prosecuting those who would vandalize graveyards like the Graf cemetery.

Then one day, while escorting a woman to her estranged husband's house to collect her sewing machine and a car, the brave young constable and the lady were gunned down by the enraged spouse. It was over twenty years since Wohlfiel had made the walk around the top of the Graf Cemetery wall, and there were those in the area who no doubt felt that the Hans Graf curse had claimed yet another victim.

Those claims might be sustained by a local newspaper reporter who, about fifty years ago, had gone to the cemetery to take some pictures for a Halloween story he was writing for his newspaper. He arrived at the cemetery at dusk, and, in order to take better advantage of the remaining daylight and get the best camera angle, climbed up on the stone wall.

However, as he was snapping his photos, he felt a "noticeable push" on his right shoulder. It was, he would later write, "not a shove, but a noticeable push, as if someone were saying 'get out of here and let me alone!'"

There was no one behind him at the time, and also no tree branches that were close enough to have blown into him as they swayed in the night wind. Prior to this incident the reporter was not a believer in ghosts and spirits, but now he says he's had second thoughts. You might say he was "pushed" into it.

NOTE: To those who visit the Hans Graf cemetery today, there is at least one other landmark in the area that lends an air of mystery to the place.

Directly across the river from the cemetery is a high stone cliff that over-looks the banks of the Susquehanna River here. The rugged stone forma-tions that make up the cliff are known locally as Schull's Rock, but to those who know the legend of the Graf Cemetery, the cliff and its stone formations may remind them of another name and place. To the more imaginative, the deep crevices and jagged pinnacles of Schull's Rocks can appear to be the ruins of an ancient castle. When viewing those ruins from the Graf Cemetery on nights when the moon is full and dark clouds hide its face, the lonely traveler might be reminded of another castle that still stands in the Carpathian Mountains of Romania.[3]

THE HAND ON THE WALL

Up until 1954, the townspeople of Jim Thorpe in Carbon County had been content with the original name of their little village. It was a name that had come down from the Indians, who must have noticed that bears liked the spot as much as they did. *Machk Tschunk*, or Bear Mountain, was the title the aborigines eventually adopted for the place, and settlers eventually corrupted that into Mauch Chunk, finally using that name for the town that grew up here.

However, in 1954, when the communities of Mauch Chunk and East Mauch Chunk agreed to merge, they agreed upon the name Jim Thorpe as the name for their new town. By a vote of ten to one, residents substituted another Indian name for the old one, deciding to honor the great Indian athlete and hero of the 1912 Olympic Games by bestowing his name upon their new borough.[4]

For over a hundred years the town of Jim Thorpe has kept that name, even though in recent years there have been suggestions that it should revert back to the original. However, most folks, in what is now the county seat of Carbon County, are content to keep the name as is, perhaps because they want their town to be remembered for something other than the infamous executions that once took place here.

---

3. Thomas Wohlfiel, interviewed by telephone, November 1, 1983; George Sheldon (born 1951), recorded January 26, 1990; George Sheldon, "Curse of the Hans Graf Cemetery," October 27, 1982, and "Ghostly Tale of a Former Skeptic," October 31, 1983, *Lancaster Intelligencer Journal*; Author not known, "Vampires and Werewolves—Frequently They Were Just Ordinary Folks With a Rare but Nasty Disease," *Lancaster Intelligencer Journal*, May 31, 1985.

4. A. Howry Espenshade, *Pennsylvania Place Names*, 148.

View of the old Mauch Chunk jail in Carbon County, where the hand on the wall can be seen.

On June 21, 1877, four men were hanged in the corridor of the Mauch Chunk jail. Each one had been convicted of murder; killings that they had carried out as part of a reign of terror inflicted upon the northeastern Pennsylvania coal regions by an organization known as the Mollie Maguires (for more information on the Mollies, and one man's interesting account of how he almost became one of their victims, see the author's story entitled "Mollie Maguire Memories," which appears in *Volume II* of this series).

The simultaneous executions drew many spectators, and the crowd continued to grow larger as the hour of execution approached. The influx was something authorities had expected, and they also had considered the possibility that the Mollies might try to rescue their friends at the eleventh hour. Consequently, the front of the jail was protected by a large contingent of fully uniformed soldiers, each carrying a large supply of ball cartridges.

The Easton Grays had very little to do that day. The executions, it turned out, went on without any disruptions. This was also the case over the next two years when there would be nine more Mollie hangings at this same spot, but the one that is remembered the most today is the hanging that occurred on March 28, 1878.

Thomas Fisher had been tried and convicted of the murder of mine boss Morgan Powell at Summit Hill in December of 1871, and now, seven years later, Fisher was preparing to meet his maker. His friend John "Yellow

Jack" Donohue had been hanged for the same crime the year before, and Fisher was about to pay the same price for his part in the murder.

However, the condemned man was not repentant, and he proclaimed his innocence to the very end, even, some say, predicting that a sign of that innocence would appear on the wall of his jail cell. Those who were there when they led Tom Fisher from cell #17 on the morning of March 28 claimed that before he left his prison cell, he made this one last statement.

"A century from now this Mauch Chunk prison will be an historical landmark," said Fisher as pointed to the wall of his cell and continued with his last words. "I am innocent. I have never entered into any conspiracy either publicly or privately to do any person any harm!"

Then, in a final act of defiance, Fisher smacked his open hand on the place on the wall where he had pointed initially and declared "If I am innocent my print will stay on that wall forever!"[5]

No one seemed to care that Thomas Fisher refused to admit his guilt, even as they led him up the steps of the scaffold. They hanged him anyway, but when an image that was unmistakably that of a man's handprint appeared on the wall

Drawing of Alexander Campbell. Is it his handprint on the wall of cell #17 in the Mauch Chunk Jail, or is it that of Thomas Fisher, or that of another Mollie? History remains undecided.

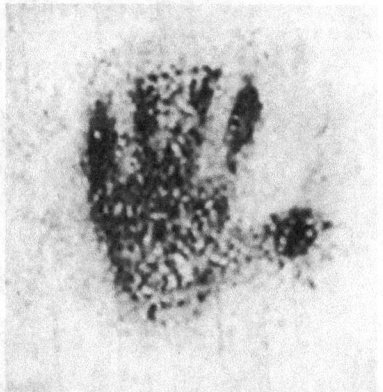

The hand on the wall at Mauch Chunk Jail. This is the best photo possible since the image on the wall is quite blurry to start with. However, it still remains as much of a mystery as when it first appeared!

5. Betty Lou McBride, "The Old Jail Museum and Molly Maguires," 8; A. Monroe Aurand Jr., *Historical Account of the Mollie Maguires*, 30–31; Chamber of Commerce, Jim Thorpe, PA, "The Mollie Maguires, Guilty or Innocent?" *Discover Jim Thorpe, PA*, 18; tourist pamphlet, "Jim Thorpe, Pennsylvania, formerly Mauch Chunk."

of cell #17 some days later, there must have been many who had second thoughts about the punishment that had been meted out to the former Mollie Maguire.

Today that handprint remains on the wall of the cell. Wardens at the jail still tell the story of a former sheriff there who, tired of the constant stream of curious onlookers, tried to remove the image. They say he tried to scrub it off, plaster it over, and hide it with numerous coats of paint.

Scaffolding inside the old Mauch Chunk jail. Replica of the scaffoldings used to hang the Mollie Maguires in the nineteenth century.

Another haunted cemetery? Eerie photo of a crow sitting on a tombstone and outlined by a cloud-covered moon. (Publication rights purchased from Shutterstock.)

When the image kept coming back the local authorities even dug away that part of the wall and filled it back up with new concrete. However, that approach didn't work either, and it appears that the jailors have decided that they can't fight what legend says is a form of justice from beyond the grave.

Historians now agree that the Mollie Maguires were tried by judges and juries that were heavily biased, reason enough for the many guilty verdicts to be overturned in the appeal processes that would be part of today's legal proceedings. This fact alone no doubt leads some to believe that the spirits of the Mollies who were unjustly executed, including Tom Fisher's, cannot rest easily.

It is Fisher's spirit, so they believe, that keeps the handprint on the Mauch Chunk jail wall of cell #17; and so to them, the supernatural explanation behind that doleful image is a reasonable one. But others who tend toward that unnatural explanation may also point to the 1975 chromatographic analysis done of the handprint by a geologist from Wilkes College in Wilkes-Barre. Results of that testing concluded that the print was actually in the wall itself rather than just on its surface. It was enough to convince many skeptics that the hand on the wall was perhaps not a hoax after all.

Nonetheless, there is some uncertainty as to whose handprint is on the wall. Some say it is Thomas Fisher's, others claim it is that of Alexander Campbell's or that of another Mollie entirely. Campbell was tried and convicted of the same crime as Fisher, so there is some connection, but there are still others who would point to the legendary world for evidence that Mauch Chunk's "hand on the wall" is nothing more than a clever publicity stunt or transplanted folklore.

For example, tales of ineffaceable incriminating marks on murderers' tombstones or ineradicable bloodstains on the floors where murder victims fell are found in many places, even here in the Keystone State. In the coal regions look no further than the town of Wiggans, where it is said that there is still a bloodstain on the floor of the house where "Black Jack" Kehoe's sister-in-law was gunned down by masked vigilantes one day. The Wiggans Patch Massacre, as it would later be referred to, was yet another murder in the continuing battle between the Mollie Maguires and the ruthless Coal and Iron Police employed by mine owners. It showed that even Kehoe, dubbed as "the King of the Mollies," was not exempt from the wrath of the unmerciful "coal kings" who owned the mines.[6]

---

6. Christine Ketusky, "The Other Side of the Mollie Maguire Coin," *Pottsville Republican Weekender*, July 17, 1971.

CHAPTER 14

A LINE MOUNTAIN
WEREWOLF

One of the finest trips I ever took, in my quests for old time Pennsylvania mountain tales and legends, took place during April of 2013. That warm and sunlit afternoon my wife and I headed into the Schwaben Creek Valley of Northumberland County to try to find some facts behind one of the strangest tales I had yet heard, in over forty years of exploring the history of all kinds of Pennsylvania mountain stories.

Although this anecdote seemed to be in a class by itself, its appeal was temporarily forgotten—an amnesia caused by the splendid countryside through which we were passing as we slowly cruised into a glorious composition of well-tended fields of green and gold, neatly kept farms with red barns and white farmhouses, an abundance of rolling hills of brown and tan, and dark blue mountains on every horizon.

Eventually, however, we were reminded of why we came; struck by the fact that despite three or four passes up and down this valley with unsurpassed scenery, we had not yet seen one flock of sheep on any hillside or in any field. The absence of sheep, we later learned, was due more to current economic factors rather than to any links with the dark tale that seemed to cast a shadow over this beautiful place; this area that seems like a paradisiacal portal to the pearly gates of heaven.

This stark contradiction was a reminder, however, that just as every dark cloud has a silver lining, many heavenly places often have dark clouds hanging over them; and that's why we wanted to know more about the incredible legend of the wolf man of Schwaben Creek Valley.

"It hasn't been here in my time," replied the young man who lived on the hill overlooking the field at the intersection of Line Mountain and Covered Bridge Roads where the wolf man was supposedly buried. We had stopped to ask him about whether or not he had ever seen the wooden grave marker that had been placed over the gravesite and on which an epitaph had supposedly been carved with the words, "*Die Wolff Mann's Graab.*"

Undeterred, despite the current resident's inability to confirm this part of the legend for us, we felt there had to be some truths behind it; we had, after all, heard the complete tale some months earlier from a valley native who had almost reached the century mark.

Ninety-four-year-old Parsett Snyder recalled seeing the sign when he was about six or seven years old, and had heard the unusual tale about it from his grandfather Aaron Snyder. The old gentleman was most gracious in sharing the story with me, but it was yet another valley native who later escorted me to the place where the young heroine of the tale had actually lived and had tended her sheep.

"The words on the grave marker meant 'the wolf man's grave' in Pennsylvania Dutch," explained Bill Paul, who was a member of the same family as that of the young heroine who figured so prominently in the tale we had heard from Parsett Snyder, "and there are still a few of us here in the valley who speak the dialect. In fact, when I was young it was hard to find anyone who could speak English! We had to learn it at school, but it's hard for me to believe that the early Pennsylvania Dutch settlers in this valley would have believed what the story says they believed; that they would have believed in werewolves!"[1]

We had to agree, but between Parsett's story and the legends from the Old Country that could have influenced the folktales and beliefs in this one, it seemed to me that there may be some reason for thinking otherwise. And so, we first turn to Parsett Snyder's account to begin the search for the truths behind the legend.

According to this former Northumberland County Justice of the Peace, sometime around 1830 or 1850, there was a family named Paul living on

---

1. Bill Paul (born 1935), interviewed July 31, 2013.

a farm that still can be found in the Schwaben Creek Valley. Among the animals raised on the farm was a flock of sheep, and its care fell on the shoulders of the Pauls' ten-year-old daughter May. It was her daily responsibility, so it seems, to shepherd the flock out of the family sheep pen and onto the nearby hillside to graze.

Little May must have looked like the Little Bo Peep of fairytale fame as she sat on the hillside with her shepherd's crook, standing guard over the docile animals. Then any fairytale-like elements of the scene began to change, one day when May noticed a strange-looking man sitting on the edge of the clearing where the sheep stood peacefully grazing. The man appeared again the next day, but other than his appearance he did not seem intimidating to the young shepherdess. In fact, she seemed to feel safer when he was around, despite his disheveled look and his unkempt long hair and beard.

He never said anything to her, and he always kept himself at a distance, so when May told her parents about her strange guardian and his non-intimidating behavior, she was surprised that they seemed indifferent about him even though they didn't even know his name.

When they no doubt explained that they thought he was just a harmless old hermit who lived in a cave on Line Mountain, it must have added to her feeling that her silent companion was helping her guard the sheep; a task she probably did not like to think about, when she heard the packs of grey wolves howl on Line Mountain after the sun seemingly set into the western shadows of Pittman Kettle every evening.

Eventually those in the nearby communities of Leck Kill and Rehbock (now spelled Rebuck) heard about May Paul's silent companion; and, along with May's parents, must have noticed something else. Almost every farm family in the valley had their own flock of sheep at that time, and virtually every one fell prey to the nocturnal forays of the grey wolves. The consequent toll on the flocks was intolerable, an economic hardship, but the Pauls' flock never seemed to suffer.

It seemed impossible, but little May Paul's charges were never harmed by the wolves; the grey marauders seemed to avoid the innocent lambs, as if repelled by some supernatural force, and so people soon began to speculate as to just what that force might be.

At this point the tale assumes its own fairytale qualities, touching on the world of werewolves and other such improbables. Nonetheless the tale claims that those who pondered the forces protecting May Paul's sheep reached the conclusion that her silent guardian was able to control the wolf packs on Line Mountain because he was a werewolf, a man who could change himself into a wolf and assume the role of the ultimate alpha male of the Line Mountain wolves as he roamed with them on their nightly forays and howled with them at the moon as it floated ghostlike in the dark skies above. They decided that it was this unlikely character that was protecting May Paul's sheep because of his fondness for her.

Despite these intimidating conclusions, a local farmer seemed unfazed by them; so when he heard the wolves howling more than usual one night on Line Mountain, he decided to take his rifle and take his chances, his fear of the unknown apparently overridden by his desire to collect the attractive bounty being offered on wolves during that same period.

He set out in the direction of the howling, and had not traveled far before seeing a black shape slinking across an open field and looking like it was staying as low to the ground as it could to conceal itself. Without further thought the man took aim and fired, convinced he was shooting at a wolf. He was sure he had hit it, even though he heard no howl of pain, but since the night had gotten considerably darker, and perhaps because he began to recall the local tales about the werewolf, he decided not to try to track the animal that night. He instead made a mental note of the place where he had shot the beast, deciding to come back the next day to follow its blood trail.

The next day, bright and early, the farmer returned to the spot where he had made his shot the night before. It did not take him long to find a blood trail and follow it to a spot in a nearby field about a mile away. As he entered the field he could see a black shape in the tall grass in the distance, and he rushed to claim his prize. However, to his horror, he found the dead body of the old hermit.[2]

There are some lurid accounts that claim the dead body of the hermit, including the palms of its hands, was covered with hair, and that its eye teeth, looking like fangs, projected out from under its upper lip, thereby

2. Parsett Snyder (born 1919), interviewed April 30, 2013 and June 11, 2013.

creating an image that resembled that of a typical werewolf as described in the vivid tales about such things. All the accounts, however, end by saying that the locals, not wanting to cause any more of a stir about the matter, kind of hushed it up, chalking it up to a hunting accident. It's also said that they buried the old hermit where he was found.[3]

That they got away with shoving the matter under the rug is not unlikely, since this area was probably outside the purview of the law back then; back in the first half of the 1800s when frontier justice may have been, judging from its remoteness even yet today, more of the norm than we realize in an isolated place like this and during those times.

Whatever the case may be, the locals, regardless of their beliefs, must have felt some remorse about the situation since they supposedly did erect the unusual marker over the man's gravesite. That the tale is still told and retold yet today lends some credence to its shocking origins. And although the grave marker no longer exists to confirm the tale, there are some other clues that can be cited as evidence of its validity.

No one today remembers the name of the wolfman nor the name of the hunter who shot him. Nor can they identify the spot where May Paul may be buried. However, the Paul farm is still a working farm today, and can be found at the corner of Schwaben Creek Road and Old State Road in Schwaben Creek Valley. The original farmhouse and barn are no longer there, replaced by modern equivalents, but the fields in back where May Paul may have tended her sheep can still be seen.

There are those who have looked into whether or not there are any county or census records that show that there was an actual person named May Paul living in Northumberland County in the 1800s. Those searches have found that the Paul farm was owned by a man named Michael Paul at that time, and one of his sons was named Tobias, who had a daughter named Lillie May. In addition, Parsett Snyder recalls that his grandfather, Aaron Snyder, claimed that he knew May Paul by sight and often saw her driving a team of horses pulling a wagonload of wool to the woolen mill in Klingerstown. That quaint old mill still stands today in Klingerstown, but it's no longer used as such, serving only for storage of odds and ends by the current owner.

---

3. John L. Moore, various newspaper articles and book: *Ghosts, Goblins, and Ghouls.*

As far as the wolves on Line Mountain, there is no doubt that they once frequented that locale judging from the local wolf tales that can still be heard about them today (see my *Volume VII* for some of those tales). Today, however, there are no packs of wolves to be found there, but instead there are packs of coyotes who have found the recesses and hollows of these hills to be just as an inviting place to stay as the wolves did in the 1800s. Locals say that they can hear the nightly howls of the coyotes much like residents must have heard the howls of the wolf two centuries ago.

The fact that there were once flocks of sheep kept by local farmers in the valley is evidenced by a local road sign leading to one of the isolated farms in the Schwaben Creek Valley. The name on the sign is Sheep Lane.

Regarding the murder of the hermit and the belief he was a werewolf, the crime itself will remain unsolved. Was the murder not an accident after all? Did locals instead decide that the hermit was stealing their sheep, or did they decide that he was pursuing May Paul for unsavory reasons? Or was it a combination of both, that, coupled with the hermit's unsavory appearance, may have led them to decide to mete out their own form of vigilante justice?

We'll never know, of course, but the werewolf part of the story may have been a touch that arose from tales from the Old Country that may still have been fresh in the minds of those early German settlers and their more gifted storytellers.

Germany is famous for its fairytales and tales of the supernatural, including those of werewolves, and there is no other tale more fascinating than that of the Wolfstone. Set somewhere in the remote valleys of eastern Germany's Fichtel Mountains next to the Czech border, the ancient account tells of a local shepherd whose flock of sheep was being systematically devoured by a large wolf. Tired of losing so many sheep, the shepherd hired a local hunter to watch for the beast and shoot it when it next appeared.

The hunter kept watch for a number of days, until one foggy night the wolf emerged from the dense forest next to the field where the sheep were pastured. Carefully taking aim, the hunter fired at the wolf several times, feeling sure that at least one bullet had been a direct hit. However, the wolf ran away as though unscathed, leaving the hunter scratching his

*Little Bo Peep? Artist's rendition of a sheperdess and her sheep. Probably
a good likeness for Lilly Mae Paul when she was tending her sheep in the
shadows of Line Mountain. (From the 1863 oil painting titled "Shepherdess
with Her Flock" by Jean-François Millet)*

head. The shepherd was just as perplexed at this strange turn of events,
until the next morning when he noticed a local hag, who had been long
suspected of witchcraft, hobbling down the street as though she had been
badly wounded.

The shepherd immediately deduced that the woman was a female werewolf who changed herself into a wolf every night so she could attack his
sheep. He immediately reported her to the authorities, who arrested her
and threw her into one of their darkest dungeons, where they chained her
to the floor. However, when they came back to interrogate her the next
morning. she had mysteriously vanished!

For two nights the hunter and the shepherd stood watch over the flock
of sheep, expecting the wolf to attack the helpless animals again. Then on
the second night the wolf came back, looking fiercer and more vengeful
than before. At first it appeared that she was going to attack the sheep once
again, but then she rushed at the shepherd.

View of the fields in back of the Paul farmhouse. The way it still looks today, with Line Mountain in the background. In the Schwaben Creek Valley, Northumberland County.

Fortunately, the hunter had a silver knife tucked in his belt and, knowing that his rifle would have no effect, pounced upon the wolf and repeatedly slashed at the animal's belly, causing it to howl in agony as it writhed upon the ground and its blood began to flow.

Shortly thereafter, it was said, the wolf turned back into its human form; that of the old witch. Deciding to take no chances, the two men buried the body of the old woman in a grave twenty feet deep, and, to sanctify the spot, marked the gravesite with a large stone cross. The cross is yet referred to today as the "Wolfstone" and it's said locals still avoid the place because of the strange events that occur there.[4]

There is yet another account from the Hartz Mountains of Germany that tells of a stranger that came there one day, offering his services to the country folk. No one knew his name, and so they referred to him as the Old Man. He was often hired to herd sheep, and he did so to everyone's satisfaction until he was hired by a man named Melle who lived near Neindorf.

---

4. Alexander Schoppner, *Legends from the Bavarian Countryside.*

The Old Woolen Mill. The same mill that Lilly May Paul came to with her wagonloads of wool. The mill still stand near Klingerstown, Schuylkill County – picture taken by the author in April of 2013.

The strange man began to pester Melle about a spotted lamb that had recently been born in his flock, repeatedly asking Melle to give it to him. Melle refused the requests, but he continued to employ the persistent fellow. Then one morning he hired the man to help shear his sheep, and then left for the day. When he returned, he found all work had been done as requested, but he noticed that his spotted lamb was missing along with the Old Man.

For many months no one saw the stranger again, but then one afternoon he paid an unexpected visit to Melle while he was grazing his sheep in the Katten Valley. The man called out to the shepherd in a sneering voice, saying that "your spotted lamb sends its greetings"![5]

Angered by the taunt, Melle grabbed his shepherd's crook to attack the thief, but when he did so the man turned into a wolf and attacked him. Melle was at first paralyzed with fright, until his pack of dogs attacked the wolf and chased it through forest and glen until they cornered it under a large rocky outcrop.

---

5. Jacob Grimm, "Werewolf Rock," *Teutonic Mythology.*

Emboldened by this turn of events, Melle attacked the wolf with unbridled fury, whereupon the wolf turned back into the Old Man, who begged for his life. His pleas went unheeded and so the man transmogrified himself into a large thorn bush, and then into a wolf once again. The many transfigurations did not stop Melle, who continued to pummel the beast until it was dead. For ages thereafter the cliff where the werewolf died was known as "Wolf Rock" or "Werewolf Rock," and is so-called yet today.[6]

There are many other such tales from the dark forests of Germany and from other European countries as well. Perhaps it was one such tale that led to embellishments of the story of the Wolf-Man's death in the Schwaben Creek Valley of Northumberland County. Unfortunately, we cannot know for sure whether that's the case or not, but it would not be the first time that elements of European folk tales crept into the folktales of this country. If that's also true in this case, then we may at least conjecture that the Schwaben Creek Valley tale, although based on an actual event, may have been embellished with European werewolf beliefs in order to make it a more entertaining story.

---

6. Ibid.

CHAPTER 15

RETRIBUTION

As readers of the previous volumes in the *Pennsylvania Fireside Tales* series may recall, there were many superstitions associated with witchcraft that lingered well into the twentieth century in some of the darker hollows, misty glens, and cloud-covered peaks of the Keystone State. The chapter titled "Driving in the Peg" in this volume recounts some of those superstitions, including the idea that a good witch, most popularly referred to as a braucher, could counteract the evil spells of a bad witch, usually referred to as a *hechs* [hex].

Since medieval times it was often the misfortune of destitute and single old crones to be suspected of witchcraft despite their innocence. Based on appearance alone, or upon a grudge held by a neighbor or family member, the unfortunate elderly women were often convicted of being a hex, the most common appellation applied to them.

The convictions oftentimes led to executions; just punishment, it was believed, for someone who had sold their soul to the devil and was therefore bound to inflict his torments upon both animals and people alike. However, these evil actions were not without risk to the perpetrators, or at least that was an idea that served as consolation to those who believed they were the victims of a hex's evil curses.

It was believed that brauchers, the aforementioned good witches, had the power to counteract evil spells, and in doing so inflict bodily harm upon the hex who had cast the spell in the first place. Such was the level of faith in the braucher's powers that it was thought that their resultant counter-hex would render the hex's spell totally ineffective, and in the process also cause its perpetrator to suffer intense pain and bodily injury.

It was an idea that, much to my surprise, I found to be still somewhat prevalent when I first started collecting my legends and folktales back in the 1970s, and little did I suspect that I would still hear tales like it even into the twenty-first century. However, in 2023 I heard one such story while sitting in a remote mountain homestead, located along an unpaved dirt byway that winds through a dreary and dimly lit defile into a mountain wilderness where many such tales were once often recalled.

The Magic Circle. This 1886 painting by John William Waterhouse depicts a witch or sorceress using a wand to draw a fiery magic circle on the Earth to create a ritual space for her ceremonial magic - from the collection of the author.

The eighty-seven-year-old mountain man, born in 1936, was eager to impart his tale, having "carried it for seventy years or better." He did so, he said, because "the relatives were living and still are. I have lots of friends around here, and I have to be careful!" Nonetheless, with my promise to conceal the family name of those involved, he agreed to share the story with me.

"I know it's true," he began, "because I went through it! Mom and dad never kept much from me, and we talked about this. My mother, Jennie Grenoble, started cryin' all night, and she couldn't stop. This was after she was married and livin' in there. We used to live at the house down from the Synagogue Church in Synagogue Gap down towards Voneida Gap. There is a house on the right where Butz Brown used to live, and our house was directly opposite on the other side of the road.

"This was probably when I was about eight years old, and this went on for quite some time. She doctored and the doctors couldn't do anything. I remember her cryin' at night still, every night and only at night, never during the day. My dad had an uncle, his name was Ab Wert, who lived in Lock Haven, and he told my dad, 'I know of a person over here who's really good with good witchcraft. Do you want me to set you up with an appointment?'

"And my dad said 'Yeah, I'll do anything,' and so he set us up with an appointment with this guy. I don't remember his name, only that he lived on a steep hill at a red light in Lock Haven. It seemed like the sessions were helping for a while. However, they would come back, even after we went over there for quite a few trips.

"And the guy finally said that my mother's problems were coming from this person, and that she couldn't be stopped without killing her. Well, dad didn't want to get into that, you know, but he didn't want this cryin' all the time either. So, the doctor said, 'I have nothing else to do unless we do the ultimate.'

"So, he told them that when they got home a neighbor of ours would have died. And on our way home, my uncle Charles Grenoble was goin' down Pine Woods Hill out there, and we stopped and talked.

"He said, 'Did you hear that Mertie L died?'

"I think the thing stopped there! We got home and sure enough, she had just dropped over. They were neighbors of ours, and that was the last

Fanciful depiction of the Salem Witch Trials. From an 1892 lithograph by Joseph E. Baker, it depicts an accused witch appearing before the court and using her supposed occult powers to send her handcuffs flying and to cause lightning to come through the window. Powers to be feared indeed, but apparently not as strong as those some believed were used by a braucher to help Mrs. Ernest Grenoble some years ago!

time my mother cried at night! I don't know to this day whether the family ever knew why Mertie died"![1]

I leave it to the reader to decide whether or not a braucher's power led to Mertie L.'s death or not, but it was her death that no doubt gave some comfort to those who thought they could rely upon such remedies to protect them from evil witches and their hexes.

NOTE: In addition to deep-rooted cultural convictions, there was also a strong religious faith that reinforced the idea that brauchers were divinely directed to counteract the spells of evil witches. The basis for that faith could be found in the Bible (King James version). In particular, the following verses:

1. Donald Grenoble (born 1936), interviewed December 08, 2023.

Mark 16 (verses 17-18): "And these signs shall follow those who believe. In my name shall they cast out devils . . . they shall lay hands on the sick, and they shall recover."

The following was sometimes called the "blood verse"[2] since it provided confirmation that brauchers had the power to stop the flow of blood gushing from an open wound:

Ezekial 16 (verse 6): "And when I passed by thee, and saw thee polluted in thine own blood, I said unto thee when though wast in thy blood, Live; yea, I said unto thee when though wast in thy blood, Live."

2. Thomas White, *Supernatural Lore of Pennsylvania*, 138.

ACKNOWLEDGMENTS

To those who are yet unborn but who may read these tales sometime in the future, may you know a Pennsylvania that is as full of colorful characters and romantic memories of the past as the Pennsylvania I found when I roamed her hills and mountains searching for these links to a storied land that will ever captivate and hold my imagination.

BIBLIOGRAPHY

Africa, J. Simpson, *History of Huntingdon and Blair Counties, Pennsylvania*, Philadelphia, Louis Everts Co., 1883.

Aldrich, Lewis Cass, *History of Clearfield County, Pennsylvania*, Syracuse, NY, D. Mason and Company, 1887.

Anderson, Barbara M., editor, *Haines Township Life and Tradition*, Haines Township Bicentennial Book Committee, Aaronsburg, PA, 1976.

Aurand, A. Monroe Jr., *Historical Account of the Mollie Maguires*, Lancaster, PA, The Aurand Press, undated.

Baughman, Ernest W., *Type and Motif-Index of the Folktales of England and North America*, Indiana University Folklore Series No. 20, The Hague, The Netherlands, Mouton and Co., 1966.

Beers, J. H. and Co., *Commemorative Biographical Record of Central Pennsylvania, Including the Counties of Centre, Clinton, Union, and Snyder*, Chicago, IL, J. H. Beers and Co., 1898.

Blackman, Emily C., *History of Susquehanna County, Pennsylvania*, Philadelphia, Claxton, Remsen and Haffelfinger, 1873.

Brendle, Thomas R., and Charles W. Unger, *Folk Medicine of the Pennsylvania Germans*, NY, A. M. Kelley, 1970 reprint.

Day, Sherman, *Historical Collections of the State of Pennsylvania*, Port Washington, NY, Ira J. Friedman, 1843, (1969 reprint).

Davis, Taring S., *A History of Blair County, Pennsylvania*, Harrisburg, PA, National Historical Association, Inc., 1931.

Egle, William H., *History of the Commonwealth of Pennsylvania*, Philadelphia, E. M. Gardner, 1883.

Espenshade, A. Howry, *Pennsylvania Place Names*, Harrisburg, PA, The Evangelical Press, 1925.

Everts and Stewart, *History of Northumberland County, Pennsylvania*, Philadelphia, Everts and Stewart, 1876.

Faris, John T., *Seeing Pennsylvania*, Philadelphia, J. B. Lippincott, 1919.

Fiske, John, *Myths and Myth-makers, Old Tales and Superstitions Interpreted by Comparative Mythology*, Boston, Houghton, Mifflin Co., 1893.

Fletcher, Stevenson W., *Pennsylvania Agriculture & Country Life, 1640–1840*, Harrisburg, PA, Pennsylvania Historical and Museum Commission, 1971.

Furnas, J. C., *The Americans, A Social History of the United States 1587–1914*, New York, NY, G. P. Putnam's Sons, 1969.

Glimm, James Y., *Flatlanders and Ridgerunners, Folktales from the Mountains of Northern Pennsylvania*, Pittsburgh, PA, University of Pittsburg Press, 1983.

Grimm, Jacob, *Teutonic Mythology*, George Bell & Sons, London, 1882.

Godcharles, Frederic A., *Pennsylvania: Political, Governmental, Military, and Civil*, New York, The American Historical Society, 1933.

Hain, H. H., *History of Perry County, Pennsylvania*, Harrisburg, PA, Hain-Moore Co., 1922.

Hanna, Charles A., *The Wilderness Trail*, New York, NY, AMS Press, 1911.

Hardwick, Charles, *Traditions, Superstitions, and Folk-lore, (Chiefly Lancashire and the North of England)*, Manchester, England, A. Ireland & Co., 1872.

Harting, James E., *Extinct British Animals*, London, Trubner and Co., 1880.

Heckewelder, Reverend John, *History, Manner, and Customs of the Indian Nations*, Philadelphia, Lippincott's Press, 1876.

Henson, Michael P., *A Guide to Treasure in Pennsylvania*, Boulder, CO, Carson Enterprises, undated.

Higgins, C. A., *Titan of Chasms: The Grand Canyon of Arizona*, Chicago, Santa Fe Press, 1906.

Hohman, John George, *Pow-wows, or Long Lost Friend*, Reading, PA, unknown publisher, 1820.

Kerlin, W. W., editor, *Centre Hall, Centre County, Pennsylvania*, Centre Hall, PA, Centre Hall Fire Co., 1942.

Klees, Frederic, *The Pennsylvania Dutch*, New York, Macmillan Co., 1971.

Korson, George, *Pennsylvania Songs and Legends*, Baltimore, Johns Hopkins Press, 1949.

———, *Black Rock, Mining Folklore of the Pennsylvania Dutch*, Baltimore, Johns Hopkins Press, 1960.

Linn, John Blair, *Annals of Buffalo Valley Pennsylvania, 1755–1855*, Harrisburg, PA, Lane S. Hart, 1877.

———, *History of Centre and Clinton Counties, Pennsylvania*, Philadelphia, Louis H. Everts Co., 1883.

Lyman, Robert R., *Amazing Indeed, Strange Events in the Black Forest*, Coudersport, PA, The Potter Enterprise, 1973.

McKnight, William J., *Pioneer Outline History of Northwestern Pennsylvania*, Philadelphia, Lippincott Co., 1905.

Meginness, John F., *History of Lycoming County, Pennsylvania*, Chicago, Brown, Runk & Co., 1892.

Meginness, John F., *Otzinachson, A History of the West Branch Valley*, Williamsport, PA, Gazette Printing House, 1889.

Meyer, Dorothy C., *Legends and Lore of Centre County*, State College, PA, self-published, 1979.

Mitchell, Edwin Valentine, *It's an old Pennsylvania Custom*, New York, Vanguard Press, Inc., 1947.

Montgomery, Thomas L., editor, *Frontier Forts of Pennsylvania, Volume I*, Harrisburg, PA, Pennsylvania Historical Commission, 1915.

Potter County Historical Society authors, *Historical Sketches of Potter County*, Coudersport, PA, Potter County Historical Society, 1976.

Reynolds, Patrick M., *Strange But True, Incredible Stories about Pennsylvania*, Willow Street, PA, The Red Rose Studio, 1978.

Rhoads, Samuel N., *Mammals of Pennsylvania and New Jersey*, Lancaster, PA, Wickersham Printing Co., 1903.

Rung, Albert, *Rung's Chronicles of Pennsylvania History*, Huntingdon, PA, Huntingdon County Historical Society, 1984.

Sassaman, Grant N., editor, *Pennsylvania, A Guide to the Keystone State*, Pennsylvania Writers' Project, New York, Oxford University Press, 1940.

Schoppner, Alexander, *Legends From the Bavarian Countryside, Out of the Mouths of the People*, Munich, Rieger Press, 1852.

Shank, William H., *The Amazing Pennsylvania Canals*, York, PA, American Canal & Transportation Center, 1960.

Shoemaker, Henry W., *Pennsylvania Wild Cats*, Altoona, PA, Altoona Tribune Publishing Co., 1916.

Sipe, C. Hale, *The Indian Chiefs of Pennsylvania*, Butler, PA, Ziegler Printing Co., 1927.

———, *The Indian Wars of Pennsylvania*, Harrisburg, PA, The Telegraph Press, 1931.

Smith, Elmer L., editor, *Logging in the Pennsylvania North Woods*, Lebanon, PA, Applied Arts Publishers, 1971.

Swetnam, George, and Smith, Helene, *A Guidebook to Historic Western Pennsylvania*, Pittsburgh, University of Pittsburgh Press, 1976.

Tome, Phillip, *Pioneer Life, or Thirty Years a Hunter*, Baltimore, MD, Gateway Press, 1989, (reprint of the 1854 edition.)

Wallace, Paul A. W., *Indians in Pennsylvania*, Harrisburg, PA, Pennsylvania Historical Commission, 1970.

White, Thomas, editor, *Supernatural Lore of Pennsylvania*, Charleston, SC, The History Press, 2014.

Williams, Harry M., *The Story of Scotia*, State College, PA, The Centre County Historical Society, 1992.

Woodcock, E. N., *Fifty Years a Hunter and Trapper*, Columbus, OH, A. R. Harding Publishing Co., 1941.

ABOUT THE AUTHOR

JEFFREY R. FRAZIER is a native of Centre Hall, Centre County. A 1967 graduate of Penn State University, BS degree in Science. He also holds an MBA in Finance from Rider University in New Jersey. He currently resides at 100 Hawknest Way, Graystone Court Villas—Apt. 135, Bellefonte, PA, 16823. He can be reached via phone at 814-360-4401, or by email at jandhfra2@yahoo.com, or by contacting his publisher (Sunbury Press).

This Sunbury Press edition of *Volume 6* of the author's *Pennsylvania Fireside Tales* series is a new edition and represents an expanded and improved version of all previous editions. Formatting has been improved, as well as number and quality of photos, but all the same tales and photos that appeared in the original editions are included in this edition, along with new details added in some cases that were obtained after the last edition was published.

www.ingramcontent.com/pod-product-compliance
Lightning Source LLC
Chambersburg PA
CBHW011159090426
42740CB00020B/3413